Here's all the great literature in this grade level of *Celebrate Reading!*

Mirror, Mirror
And Other Reflections

Book A Celebrate Reading!

Triumph of the Human Spirit
Meeting Challenges

Book B Celebrate Reading!

Out of the millions who were silenced forever, one voice remains to remind us—the voice of

Anne Frank
The Diary
of a Young Girl

Featured Poets
Langston Hughes
Eve Merriam
Tony Moreno

Without a Map
Searching for Who You Are

Book C Celebrate Reading!

You Have Seen Our Faces

Stories About America

The Promised Land
from the book by Mary Antin

I Have a Dream
by Martin Luther King, Jr.

Always to Remember: The Story of the Vietnam Veterans Memorial
from the book by Brent Ashabranner
✳ ALA Notable Children's Book

Featured Poets
Walt Whitman
Emma Lazarus
Carl Sandburg

More Great Books to Read!

Queen of Hearts
by Vera and Bill Cleaver

Julie of the Wolves
by Jean Craighead George

After the Dancing Days
by Margaret Rostkowski

Prairie Songs
by Pam Conrad

Jacob Have I Loved
by Katerine Paterson

The Upstairs Room
by Johanna Reiss

The Mouse Rap
by Walter Dean Myers

Shark Beneath the Reef
by Jean Craighead George

TITLES IN THIS SET

The Cover Story
The cover and title pages were done in
watercolor and ink by Marc Rosenthal. Marc
has always been interested in art and was
encouraged by his father who was a designer.
He studied architecture in college but soon
decided that the freedom and creativity of art
were more interesting for him.

ISBN: 0-673-80081-4

Copyright © 1993
Scott, Foresman and Company, Glenview, Illinois
All Rights Reserved.
Printed in the United States of America.

Acknowledgments appear on page 144.

45678910RRS99989796959493

MIRROR, MIRROR

AND OTHER REFLECTIONS

ScottForesman
A Division of HarperCollinsPublishers

CONTENTS

WHAT'S IN A NAME?

What Do I Do Now?

by Ellen Conford

Dear Dr. Lamour,
I never thought I'd be writing to you about romantic problems. Since I've never had any romance to speak of, I never had any romantic problems to write to you about.

But here I am, writing to you because you've helped so many people and I really don't have anyone to turn to in my time of need. Which this is.

Actually, I don't have a romantic problem yet. The problem is that I don't have a *romance* yet. And I want one. A particular one, that is.

His name is Alvin. He sits next to me in geometry—my worst subject! He never says a word to me. Sometimes he nods when I sit down in the morning, but that's about it. The thing is, I think I'm madly in love with him and I don't know what to do about it.

I know it's probably hard to believe that I could be madly in love with someone named Alvin, but "What's in a name?" as Shakespeare said. (I think it was Shakespeare. It may have been Gertrude Stein.)

Anyway, I am an extremely shy person, and since he never speaks to me, I don't know how to get him interested, even if he *could* be interested in me, which he might be if I could only say something witty or clever, which he would have to answer or, at least, smile at.

So far all I've been able to do is say hi, and that hasn't exactly bowled him over, and why should it, because hi is not a very witty or clever remark. (That's when he just sort of nods.)

Anyway, I don't know what to do about this. If he didn't sit right next to me, I guess I would just worship him from afar, but he's not afar, he's right there, and who knows what might happen if I could just get him talking?

So my question really is, I guess, how do you get a boy who never talks to you to talk to you, when you haven't got anything to say to him except, "I'm madly in love with you," which, of course, I could never say. I mean, I'm *really* shy.

Hopefully yours,
Extremely Shy Person

Dear Extremely Shy Person,

I'll bet Alvin is every bit as shy as you are! I'll bet that's why he hasn't said anything to you. For all you know, he's as interested in you as you are in him! But you'll never know if neither of you ever tries! Since you're having trouble with geometry, why not work up your courage and ask him to help you with the homework? That gives you a good excuse to "break the ice" and talk to him. He might just be waiting for you to make the first move! And, as a bonus, you might even learn geometry!

Dr. Lamour

Dear Dr. Lamour,
　　　　　You remember I wrote to you about Alvin, the boy who sits next to me in geometry? You told me to ask him to help me with my homework, since I am so bad at geometry.

Well, that may have sounded like an easy thing to do. I mean, it was a very ingenious and sensible suggestion, because if I asked him a direct question like that, I knew he'd have to answer. And if he just nodded, like he usually does, that would mean yes!

But, remember, I am very shy and not good at talking to people, and when you said I should "work up my courage," you said it exactly right. Because that's what I had to do.

Three days in a row I went into class, sat down next to Alvin, and tried to open my mouth to say, "Boy, I really need help in geometry. Could you help me?"

Finally, on the fourth day, I gave myself this really stern "pep talk" before geometry, and I went in and sat down next to Alvin, and was just about to "take the plunge" when Ms. Fromberg, our teacher, handed back Monday's test papers.

I got a 52 and thought, This is it, this is the perfect chance to ask Alvin for help. So I turned around to talk to him, and saw, just before he stuffed it into his notebook, *his* test paper, with a big 36 circled in red at the top.

What do I do now?

Hopelessly yours,
Extremely Shy Person

Dear ESP,

The situation isn't as hopeless as it seems! After all, since Alvin is doing as badly in geometry as you are, you have something in common! That's a "plus" in any relationship. And misery loves company, you know! Why not tell Alvin about the trouble you're having with this subject? Then he'll probably tell you about his problems with it, and before you know it, you've got the conversational ball rolling!

Dr. Lamour

Dear Dr. Lamour,
I don't know if you remember me, but I wrote you about this boy I'm madly in love with who's also failing geometry and you told me to talk to him about my trouble with geometry to start the "conversational ball rolling."

Well, the most awful thing happened!

When I came home from school the day I got the 52 on the last test, my parents got really upset, and when we figured out my average, we realized I would probably fail for the marking period, so my parents got me a tutor.

And the tutor is really good—better than my teacher, in fact—and she's been working with me for three weeks now and wouldn't you know it? All of a sudden, all those things I didn't understand, I started to understand. It was just like in the cartoons, when a light bulb goes on over a person's head.

So on the last two quizzes we had, I got a 9 and a 10. (Which is the same as 90 and 100 on a big test.) So now I can't talk to Alvin about how badly we're both doing in geometry because I'm doing great, and if misery loves company, I can't be company for him anymore.

I have the rottenest luck in the world!

Now Alvin looks at my test papers, and his test papers, and just sighs and sticks his in his notebook. He probably hates me!

I don't know *what* to do now!

Despairingly yours,
Extremely Shy Person

Dear Extremely,

You could be of great help to Alvin in his time of need. Sometimes the best way to get over your own shyness is to help someone else who needs help.

Since Alvin has noticed how well you've been doing in geometry, why don't *you* offer to help *him?* He'll be doubly grateful: not only for the help you can give him but for showing that you're interested and you care.

Just work up your courage and try it! Good luck!

Dr. Lamour

Dear Dr. Lamour,
It's me again.
I'm sorry to keep bothering you like this, but really, everything seems to go wrong for me, and I just don't know who else to turn to.

I mean, it's not bad enough that I'm an extremely shy person, it's not bad enough that I'm now passing geometry, it's not bad enough that I fell madly in love

with someone who will probably never be interested in me, but to top it all off, I read these letters you get from people who are so grateful for the help you've given them and tell you their whole lives have changed because of your advice, and I wonder, How come you give me such good advice and nothing ever works?

Remember how you told me to talk to Alvin about how well I was doing in geometry now because of the tutor? Well, like you said, I "worked up my courage." (That took two days. And on the third day, I had to give myself another pep talk.)

Anyway, the third day I was determined to talk to Alvin, especially since we got another quiz handed back, and I got a 10 and Alvin got a 3.

So before he could hide his paper away in his notebook, I took a deep breath and said, "You know, I was doing really rotten in geometry, too. And then my parents got me a tutor, and I've gotten 9's and 10's on all the quizzes ever since."

And Alvin finally said something to me.

You know what he said?

"Must be a very good tutor."

I was so excited that he was talking to me at last that I just blurted out, "Oh, she is, she's terrific. Much better than Ms. Fromberg."

And he said, "Could you give me her phone number?"

What could I do?

I gave him her phone number.

Why am I doing everything wrong? Why isn't this working out like you said? You give such good advice to everybody else, what's the *matter* with me?

And what in the world should I do *now?*

Desperately yours,
Extremely Shy Person

Dear Person,

There is nothing the matter with you that a little self-confidence wouldn't cure! You don't really need a "gimmick" to get a boy to pay attention to you. You just have to be brave enough to take the risk of showing that *you're* interested in *him*. Your mutual difficulties with geometry made a good starting point, but it's not the *only* starting point.

There's more than one way to "skin a cat." Or start a relationship. Why not give a party and invite Alvin? Why not ask his opinion on the upcoming elections? And there's still geometry. You might even suggest studying together, now that you're both working extra hard on it.

You give up too easily!

Dr. Lamour

Dear Dr. Lamour,
I know it's been a long time since I wrote to you, and I really meant to write sooner to thank you for all your help and advice about my problem, namely Alvin who sits next to me in geometry.

You were very patient about answering all my letters and giving me such good suggestions. I'm really grateful that you took all that time and trouble with my "small" problem, when there are so many people out there who write to you about divorces and alcoholism and compulsive gambling.

But I did want to let you know what happened, because I thought, Who knows? Maybe someone else with the same problem will see my letter if you print it, and realize what Dr. Lamour can do to help *them*.

Well, after my last letter to you I thought about the advice you gave me. As I am an extremely shy person, I was afraid that giving a party and asking Alvin to come when we'd hardly ever exchanged two words to each other might seem a little pushy, and besides, to tell you the truth, I didn't have the nerve.

I guess I was afraid if I did invite him, and he said no, I'd be so embarrassed and upset I wouldn't be able to concentrate in geometry for the whole rest of the year, what with him sitting right next to me and me knowing he didn't like me. And now that I'm running an 85 average in geometry, I'd really hate not to be able to concentrate in class!

Then I thought about your suggestion that we discuss the elections, and I realized that if I asked his opinion about the candidates, and he told me, I'd have nothing to say back, because I didn't know the first thing about the elections, except that everybody says that one of the candidates for state senate from our district is a crook, but that's only political mudslinging, I suppose. But the thing is, I really wasn't interested in the elections, which I suppose is very irresponsible and un-American, but I'm too young to vote anyway, so I just didn't get involved. How could I start a discussion on a topic I couldn't discuss?

That left studying geometry together.

Well, if I couldn't work up the courage to ask Alvin to a party where there'd be not just him but lots of other people, I certainly didn't have the nerve to ask him to come to my house and study geometry with me. Alone! I mean, I just *couldn't*.

But that gave me an idea.

My tutor, Mrs. Lee, was helping me prepare for the midterm exam, going over all the stuff that I'd been failing in the first few weeks of the semester, when I asked her if Alvin had ever called her.

She said yes he had, and she'd seen him three times already.

So I said, "He's sort of nice, don't you think?"

And she said yes, but kind of introverted. (So I guess you were right about him being as shy as I am!)

And I told her maybe she hadn't noticed, but I was really introverted, too.

So she said, "Yes, I noticed," and sort of smiled. She's really a very sweet person, along with being a terrific tutor.

And then this light bulb went on over my head again.

"You must be very busy this time of year," I said, "what with everybody cramming for midterms and all."

And she said she was, and it was hard to arrange her schedule to accommodate everyone.

"Well," I said, "you could double up. I mean, like, for instance, Alvin and I are in the same class, and we're studying for the same midterm, so you could tutor us both in the same hour and make the same amount of money in one hour instead of two."

And she sort of grinned again and tilted her head and asked, "You think that would be fair? The point of a tutor is to provide one-to-one instruction."

And I said, "Yes, I know, but you've been such a good tutor, you can see I don't need that much help anymore. With *geometry*, anyway."

Her eyes kind of twinkled knowingly. And she thought about it for a little while, and then said, "Well, I guess it would be all right just *once*."

"Just once is all I want," I said.

So she set up a session at her house, telling Alvin it was necessary this one day that she work with two students at the same time. He told her he didn't mind because he was doing so much better since she'd been tutoring him, and if the *other* student needed more help than he did, that would be okay.

It wasn't till he got to her house that he realized the other student was me!

Mrs. Lee sat us side by side at her dining room table and gave us some proofs to do, and told us if either of us got stuck we could ask the other for help, and to see if we could work out the problem together.

Neither of us got stuck on the first two proofs. By the third one, I was getting a little worried. Alvin still hadn't said anything to me except a kind of startled hi when he walked in the door and saw me. This whole hour could be wasted if something didn't happen soon.

I looked sideways at him. He was staring down at the third problem. Just staring. His pencil wasn't moving. I looked at the proof. And then I got this weird feeling that *he* was staring sideways at *me*.

"Boy," I said nervously, "this is a tough one."

Alvin cleared his throat and mumbled something.

"Maybe we ought to work together on this one?" I said it fast but in such a little, timid whisper I didn't think he heard me.

"Okay," he said. "It's really hard."

So we started working on it, and all of a sudden we found we were talking to each other, telling each other how to do the proof!

And we started laughing, and I finally gasped, "I really knew how to do that problem."

And Alvin was laughing so hard he nearly tilted his chair over backwards onto the floor, and he said, "So did I!"

Anyway, it's not exactly a "big romance" yet, since Alvin and I are both very shy people, as you know, but things look very promising. We're studying together almost every day (without Mrs. Lee!) and I think Alvin really likes me, although of course he's too shy to come right out and say anything very romantic. But that's okay, because so am I!

I just wanted to tell you what a big help you've been and how I never could have done it without you! It's good to know I can turn to you whenever I have a problem and know that you'll help me out, no matter how many times I have to write to you and vice versa.

Gratefully yours,
Extremely Shy (but happy!) Person

Dear Ex,

I'm always delighted to be of help. But do me a favor? Next time, try Mrs. Lee first.

Dr. Lamour

Thinking About It

You are Dr. Lamour. Give advice to a completely shy person.

You have to figure out character by letters. Describe Dr. Lamour. Describe ESP. If they appeared in a TV show, what would they look like and do?

Hiram Doodlethorpe is writing an advice column. What problem will he write about, and how will he answer it?

I'VE GOT NEWS FOR YOU, G.G. THE TITLE'S ON THE BACK, TOO.

Alias Mac Detroit

by Ellen Conford

I was just standing there, minding my own business, when G. G. Graffman wheeled her bike right into Bookathon and ruined my life.

"You can't bring that bike in here, G. G.," I said. "You have to leave it outside."

She stood there stubbornly holding onto the seat, her Orphan Annie hair looking as if it would burst into flame at any moment. "I can't leave it outside; it'll get stolen."

"Lock it on the bike rack."

"I can't. Somebody stole my lock."

"Somebody stole your lock and left your bike?" I asked incredulously.

"Look, Hobie, it's taking longer to argue about this than it would for me to buy my book. Your grandfather won't mind."

"All right, all right, but hurry up. You're blocking the whole magazine rack."

G. G. nudged the kickstand down with her foot and sprinted past the Flaming Desire romances. In her gray warm-up jacket and pants she looked exactly the same from the back as she did from the front, except her toes were pointing the wrong way.

It was five o'clock. Even though the rest of the Million Dollar Mall was still humming there wasn't anyone else in my grandfather's store, so I supposed it didn't matter about the bike. I shrugged, forgot about G. G., and went back to reading the newest Mac Detroit book.

It was really good. It was called *Terminate with Extreme Pain,* and I was just at the spot where the beautiful Eurasian girl skulks into Mac's hotel room with a dagger in her teeth when . . .

"Hobie? Can I pay for this now?"

I looked up, startled, almost expecting to see the girl in the slinky black satin dress, but it was only G. G., gazing at me with her big green eyes.

She had nice eyes, I had to admit that. But that was about it, appeal-wise.

She held up the back of the book. "Don't look at the title, okay?"

"How can I tell how much it costs if I don't look at the cover?"

"The price is on the back too. See, right down there. Five ninety-five."

"I've got news for you, G. G. The title's on the back too."

"Oh." She dropped the book on the counter and made a big show of searching her jacket pocket for money.

Now, we bookstore people are trained never to bat an eyelash or make a comment on the books our customers buy unless it's a perfectly ordinary purchase like a cookbook or the latest best-seller, something like that. I mean, I'd worked in my grandfather's store for a year and I've seen people buy books you wouldn't believe.

There was the sweet little old lady who bought a copy of *The Art of Sensual Massage* and the hulking fullback type who had me ring up *Jane Fonda's Workout Book.* Then there was the mother with the screaming three-year-old twins who bought *Killer Karate from A to Z.* Come to think of it, maybe that last one wasn't such a bizarre choice.

Anyhow, you get the idea. I never make a comment, never embarrass the customer, just take the money or write up the charge slip; that's it.

Which is what I did with G. G.'s book. Even though it was called *How to Make Men Crazy* and I wanted to fall down laughing on the floor.

Mr. Cool. Take the six dollars and ten cents, slip the book in a green Bookathon bag, throw in the free bookmark.

"Thank you very much. Have a nice day."

"Do you *mean* it, Hobie?"

"Mean what? Have a nice day? Sure I mean it. Even though it's evening already."

"You say that to everybody."

"*Everybody* says that to everybody, G. G. I was just being polite."

"That's what I thought." She seemed a little dejected. "Well, see you."

She wheeled the bike out, holding the green bag in her teeth, and I went back to Mac Detroit.

Only I couldn't concentrate.

The last book in the world you'd expect G. G. Graffman to buy was *How to Make Men Crazy.* The girl was born with a microscope in her hand; her first words were "marine biology," and her idea of dressing up was to tie the laces on her Nikes. Every time she came to the store she bought stuff like *Plankton: Mysterious Denizen of the Deep*, or *Analyze Seawater in Your Own Back Yard*. For light reading I figured she relaxed with *Killer Shrimp from Outer Space*.

Once she came in and asked if we had anything new in her field and I suggested *Venus on the Half Shell* by Kilgore Trout. She looked at me kind of blankly for a minute, then said, "No, I'm not into clam mythology."

The girl is bright, but she has no sense of humor.

Anyway, the last thing you'd expect G. G. to have on her mind was driving men crazy. Now, Darlene DeVries—she's another kettle of fish.

Darlene DeVries didn't need a book to tell her how to drive men crazy. Darlene could have written the book. She didn't come into the store too often, but she was in my English class in school, and she drove me crazy for forty-two minutes every day.

She sat two desks in front of me and had this habit of tossing her long, silky-blonde hair back and hitting my friend, Nate, in the face with it. This drove *Nate* crazy, because he kept getting her hair in his eyes and mouth, along with, as he said, "God knows what else."

I said I'd change places with him in a minute, so the next day we did, but Mr. Schulman made me take my assigned seat, and I never did get to feel Darlene's hair sweep across my face.

I looked at my watch. It was five forty-five. In fifteen minutes Jennifer, a college student, would take over and my grandfather would drive me home, have dinner, and go back to the store. I couldn't believe I'd been thinking about G. G. for half an hour. (With maybe five minutes for Darlene, which just goes to show you how an unexpected event can mess up your priorities.)

What had G. G. meant when she asked, "Do you mean it?"? Who means it when he says, "Have a nice day"? And why did she look so disappointed when I said

I was just being polite? I couldn't concentrate on Mac Detroit and the beautiful Eurasian assassin. G. G. was driving me nuts.

Aha! *How to Make Men Crazy* was working already. She'd only bought it half an hour ago, and already G. G. was driving one man crazy: namely me.

Then I think I turned pale. I may even have clutched at my throat but I can't swear to it.

Was it possible, I wondered, as my sweat glands shifted into overdrive, that G. G. was out to make *me* crazy? Why else the weird question about my sincerity? If she wasn't about to hit on me, why should she care if my "Have a nice day" was heartfelt or prerecorded?

I never would have thought you could be flattered and nauseous at the same time. Until that moment.

"Oh, I don't know," Nate said. "She's not so bad. I mean, nothing to get sick over."

It was Saturday evening and we were at my house waiting for Pizza on Parade to deliver two extra-cheese specials.

"I didn't mean really sick," I said. "It's just—well, you know. Me and the Empress of Algae? What did I ever do to interest G. G.? Assuming she's interested, God forbid."

"Beats me," Nate said. "But what would Darlene DeVries want with you either?"

"She could use me as a scatter rug," I said fervently. "A lapdog, a bookend, whatever—I don't care— anything she wants."

"Look at this, sports fans!" Nate said in his announcer voice. "I think—I think—YES! A little bit of drool is trickling down the corner of his lip, a look of intense longing is coming into his eye—"

"Oh, shut up, Nate," I said impatiently. "What am I going to do?"

"Hobe, let me break this to you gently. You don't have to do anything, because nothing's happened yet. Did G. G. get herself gift-wrapped and delivered to your house? Did she attack you in the store? Did she Krazy-Glue herself to you in Social Studies? No, right? If you were a lobster—well, that would be another kettle of fish. Ho ho."

"Ho ho," I said sourly. "Dire things are about to happen to me, Nate. I can feel it. That girl is after me, she's studying how to make men crazy, and I'm going to be her first victim."

"Even if you're right," Nate said, "and I'm not for one minute agreeing with you, there *is* one last tiny shred of comfort you can cling to."

"What's that?"

"She's a *very* good student."

Sometimes my father gets impatient with me.

Occasionally I can sort of see his mood in perspective, because at times my grandfather gets very impatient with my father, especially when my father gets impatient with me.

But my grandfather isn't around all the time and my father is, and I've found that on an average of three days a week I can be sure I'm going to disappoint him. Somehow.

Usually it's because I have no "goals." At least, no long-term goals, as my father puts it. (I had short-term goals, mostly involving Darlene, but I didn't think they would interest my father. My grandfather, maybe.)

Ever since I turned fourteen, my father has been asking me what I want to do with my life.

How do I know? My father wants me to start thinking about choosing a college. Right now I'd like to make it through ninth grade.

My father says, "But don't you want to be *anything?* Haven't you any *idea* about a career?" My grandfather argues with him, my mother argues with him, but it never does any good. I used to keep telling him I was still a kid, and he'd say, "Sure, you're a kid when it's convenient, but when you want something you're practically all grown up."

This seemed irrelevant to me, but I finally figured out that the only way to deal with the pressure was to say something—anything—when he gave me the third degree. Like, for instance, "Oh, yeah, I decided I want to be a computer programmer."

A couple of days later he'd ask if I checked out the computer facilities at school, or if I'd looked through any college catalogues, and I'd say, "Yeah. I don't think that's for me. I'm not that good in math anyway. I'm thinking about law."

It holds him off for a while, and at least makes him think I'm taking my future as seriously as he does, which I guess is all he wants. My grandfather caught on pretty quickly to what I was doing, but my grandfather's pretty shrewd, and he sees me almost as much as my parents do.

The Bookathon store is what Grandpa calls his "Dream," and what my father calls his "crazy fantasy." He used to be an investment analyst. I guess he wasn't a very good one, because he and Grandma were never rich. When he retired he took most of the money he saved up and bought the bookstore. He owns it, but it's part of a big chain, so it's not exactly the bookstore of his dreams, which would be cozy and old-fashioned and not in the Million Dollar Mall. But he says you have to go with the times.

He hired me to help him last year because he said I was mature for my age and responsible—he said that right in front of my father, who doesn't share his opinion—and because he can pay me below the minimum wage. I don't know if he really meant that last part, but I needed the money and Grandpa knew I did.

Once, when my father was pestering me, I said, "Maybe I'll own a bookstore, like Grandpa's," and I thought he would turn purple. He was practically on the phone, ready to scream, "See what kind of an influence you are?" to his father when I said, "Joke, Dad. Just my little joke. I know there's no money in bookstores."

"That kind of joke," my mother said, "can cause cardiac arrest."

I decided what I wanted to be when I was twelve and started reading the Mac Detroit books. I wanted to be Mac Detroit—quick on the trigger, fast with the women, living hard and playing hard, facing death and danger at every corner, prowling the seamy underbelly of society in search of killers, thugs, secret agents, and dope smugglers.

At first I was more interested in the bullets Mac was dodging than the women he wasn't, but when I turned thirteen, I found the guns and the girls equally engrossing.

I realized that Mac Detroit was an adolescent fantasy written by a man named Mike Spain, who probably wouldn't know the difference between an international vice ring and the Kiwanis Club. I understood that wanting to become another Mac Detroit was *my* adolescent fantasy. But my father is very big on what he calls "role models," and when he pressed me to pick out someone I admired and strive to be like that person, I always thought of Mac Detroit.

This is not something I can tell my father, who owns an insurance agency and who, when he talks about "role models," really means "Why can't you be like me?"

I admire my father—within reason. He works out at a gym twice a week and is in great condition. He bought me all the equipment I wanted to start weight training, and taught me how to do lifts and curls and bench presses. He planned a whole body-building program for me.

But I don't want to be like him. Even though he's in better shape than Mac Detroit.

When the pizzas arrived that Saturday evening and we were all sitting at the kitchen table dividing them up, my father started in on Nate.

"So, Nate, I suppose you've begun to make college plans."

Nate was eyeing the pizzas the way I looked at Darlene. "I guess you could say that." I knew he was dying to sink his teeth into meatballs, onions, and cheese, but he restrained himself. "My plan is not to go."

"Not go to college?" My mother looked surprised.

"What kind of career can you have without a degree?" my father asked.

Nate fought with a twelve-inch strand of cheese. "I'm going to be a sportscaster. You know, like Marv Albert."

My father seemed at a loss for words. But only for a moment.

"Is that—um—a very realistic possibility? Career-wise?"

"Gee, I don't know, Mr. Katz. But that's what I want to be."

My father chewed silently for a while, then said, "Well, at least you know your own mind."

My mother sighed. "Roger, don't start."

"I know what I want to be," I said firmly. "I've made up my mind. A marine biologist." I don't know why I said that. I guess talking about G. G. before the pizzas came had given me the idea.

Nate began to choke on his pizza. His face was bright red and I knew he was just laughing and trying not to spit meatballs and onions over everything, but my parents were pretty alarmed.

"It's okay," he gasped. "I think an anchovy got stuck in my throat."

My mother frowned. "I specifically told them no anchovies."

"I guess one must've swum in by mistake."

"A marine biologist." My father had this sort of hopeful look in his eyes. I really surprised him with that one. Myself, too.

"Have you—"

"Most of the top schools are in California," I said. I guess G. G. must have told me that once.

"California!" My mother didn't seem pleased at all.

Suddenly it was as if my father snapped back to reality.

"Don't worry about it, Elaine. Next week he'll change his mind again."

Nate jabbed me in the ribs. "By next week," he whispered, "a marine biologist may be studying *you*. Stay tuned, sports fans."

After the pizzas my mother drove Nate and me to the mall so we could go to the movies. They have this big theater called The Million Dollar Multiplex and they show twelve separate movies, so there's always something to see.

There was a really long line in front of the ticket window. We had plenty of time to decide which theater to go to.

MacDetroit... FACING DEATH AND DANGER AT EVERY CORNER.

"*Fiery Fists of Death* or *The Young Cutthroats*," Nate said. "A tough decision."

"*The Young Cutthroats* is rated 'R,'" I pointed out. "They won't let us in."

"You don't think we can pass for seventeen?"

"We never have yet. There are ten other movies to choose from, Nate."

"Not when you got a Disney, a ballet movie, a doctor movie, a—holy cow, sports fans, look who's coming our way and ready to play."

"Who? Where?" I demanded.

"Here she comes, bringing the ball up court, flanked by her two teammates. She moves right to avoid a stroller, she moves left to avoid a trash can—"

It was Darlene DeVries.

"Boy, I'd like to hear what my colleague in the booth thinks about this development. Whaddya say, Horrible Hobe?"

"Shut up, will you? Just cool out."

"You heard it here first, fans, Horrible Hobie's incisive analysis. And another first, viewers. This is the first time in my long and distinguished broadcasting career that I've seen a sports announcer fall hopelessly in love with one of the players."

"*Stop it!*" My voice sounded like I was strangling. For a minute I thought I'd swallowed my tongue.

"Hi, Hobie," Darlene said, as she got behind us on line. "Going to the movies?"

Let me be the first to admit, here and now, that Darlene DeVries is not one of your world-class intellects. Let me also admit that I didn't care if her I.Q. was in single digits.

Her friends, Lesley Parker and Shawna Shepherd, stood on either side of her.

Nate turned around. "Actually, we're here for the Harvest Prune Festival. They pick a Miss Prune and everything. Aren't you one of the contestants?"

Darlene giggled.

"No, I guess you're not wrinkled enough. Wrinkles are one of the major requirements for Miss Prune. Along with the talent competition."

Darlene giggled again, although Shawna and Lesley ignored Nate.

"Cut it out," I said under my breath. "Stop making her laugh."

"You want me to make her cry?"

"I just want—"

"What movie are you going to see?" Darlene asked us. Shawna and Lesley looked bored.

"We can't decide between—" Nate began.

"What movie are *you* going to see?" I cut in.

"*Toujours Jeté,*" Darlene said. That was the ballet movie.

"What a coincidence! So are we."

Nate yelped, like he was in pain. He grabbed my arm and pulled me forward as the line inched toward the ticket window. "Are you crazy? I'm not going to see any *ballet* movie. I wouldn't be caught dead—"

"Forget the movie," I said, out of the corner of my mouth. "We can sit next to them. I'll take Darlene and you can have Shawna and Lesley."

"I don't want Shawna and Lesley!" Nate exploded. *"Keep your voice down!"*

But it really wasn't necessary, because behind us the three girls began to giggle and talk in loud, chirpy voices like they were trying to make people notice them.

I glanced over my shoulder and saw that Warren Adler and two of his obscenely tall basketball teammates had just gotten into line behind the three girls.

Obviously the girls were showing off for Warren and his friends, and I began to get a little tense. Warren was a junior, and Darlene only a ninth-grader, and although a school superstar might not be interested in a fourteen-year-old under ordinary circumstances, Darlene was no ordinary fourteen-year-old.

On the other hand, it was unlikely that Warren would spend cash money to see *Toujours Jeté,* no matter how many times he'd heard that ballet was just as athletic as any sport. I might still have a chance to sit with Darlene, who, under ordinary circumstances, would probably never sit with me if there was a chance she could sit next to Warren Adler.

By this time we were finally at the ticket window.

"Two for *Fiery Fists of Death,*" Nate said.

"Two for *Toujours Jeté,*" I said at the same time.

"You want four tickets?" the woman asked.

"No, just two," said Nate. *"Fiery Fists of Death."*

"Toujours Jeté," I whispered. I wasn't crazy about anyone knowing I was going to a ballet movie either, and any minute now people would start wondering who was holding up the line.

"Make up your mind," the woman said. "Which is it?"

Drastic times call for drastic measures. Mac Detroit wouldn't have thought twice about it and neither did I. There was a brief scuffle as I grabbed Nate's neck in a hammerlock and clamped my hand over his mouth. "I'm paying," I said, "so it's *Toujours Jeté.*"

She punched out two tickets to Theater Six. Nate threatened to punch me out. I paid for the tickets and walked extremely slowly toward the ticket taker. I was waiting for Darlene to catch up with us.

Darlene and her friends were walking extremely slowly also, until Warren Adler and his cronies had paid for their tickets.

Nate was rubbing his neck and making death threats. I paid no attention.

The candy counter was swarming with kids. Nate indicated by a low snarl that he wanted popcorn, which was okay with me, because Darlene, Shawna, and Lesley decided to buy popcorn too, after the basketball players got in the popcorn line.

At last all eight of us had popcorn. I followed Darlene toward Theater Six. Darlene followed Warren, and for one awful moment I thought she had double-crossed me and decided to go to whatever movie Warren was going to, but Warren and his friends went into Theater Five, where *Fiery Fists of Death* was playing, and Lesley just giggled, "See you later," as the team disappeared.

Darlene kept moving.

"Follow her," I whispered. Nate was hurling popcorn into his mouth with wild and reckless swoops of his arm.

"I'm going to rip your throat out," he said, popcorn spurting between his lips.

The audience for the ballet movie was pretty thin, which didn't surprise me, so I knew we could be near Darlene and her friends wherever they sat.

I lingered by the door with Nate, watching them debate over seats, ready to move down the aisle the minute they agreed.

Nate scarfed down popcorn and made plans to barbecue my liver for his dog.

"There they go," I said. "Down there. Let's move."

I gave him a little shove, and he started clumping down the aisle, leaving a trail of popcorn that crunched under my sneakers.

The lights went down and we slipped into the row behind Darlene. The movie started with a shot of a toe shoe twirling in a blue mist, with the "Blue Danube" waltz playing in the background.

Nate punched me in the biceps.

"OW!"

Darlene, Shawna, and Lesley turned around.

"Oh, hi, Hobie," Darlene said.

"Hi there." I tried to sound as if I wasn't writhing in pain. "Fancy meeting you here."

Darlene giggled. Lesley and Shawna turned back to the screen.

"Hi, Nate," Darlene said.

Nate growled.

Ten minutes into the movie, Shawna scampered up the aisle. A few minutes later she trotted back and sat down. The three girls held a whispered conference; the only thing I could make out sounded like "No one's there now."

A minute later Darlene, Lesley, and Shawna slipped out of their seats and headed back up the aisle.

"Probably getting more candy," I told Nate. "They'll be right back." I hoped I was right—but I had a funny feeling the girls were not going to get candy. They still had their popcorn boxes. And they'd taken their jackets.

Ten more minutes went by. It seemed longer, but that may have been because of all the ballet I was sitting through.

"They're not coming back," I said finally, defeated. "They must have sneaked into Five."

Nate turned my way for the first time and looked directly at me, his eyes glittering in the dark. "You mean, I am sitting here watching fairy princesses hop around on their toes *for no reason at all?* Is that what you're trying to tell me?"

"If they could sneak into the other theater, we probably could too. Come on."

Nate actually smiled.

First we walked all the way around the twelve theaters to the bathroom, where we hung out for a couple of minutes. This was so no one would see us walk right out of Six and into Five. That didn't seem very likely, because the only usher around was flirting with the girl at the candy counter, but there was no point in taking chances.

"Look nonchalant," I advised, as we strolled out of the men's room and past theaters Twelve through Seven. Nate nodded and tried to whistle.

No sound came out, but a lot of popcorn did.

There was no usher outside Theater Five, so we eased the door open and slid in. Theater Five was mobbed, and no wonder. On the screen two Oriental guys were trying to tap-dance on each other's teeth, and the grunts, screams, and general sound effects were terrific. Everybody was yelling and cheering.

"Oh boy!" said Nate. "Oh boy!"

I just had time to wonder how come they didn't call the movie *Fiery* Feet *of Death* when an usher in a red jacket, who had cunningly concealed himself in a little niche between the last row of seats and the door, stepped between us.

"Out!"

"Hey, wait a minute," I protested.

"Out. You weren't in this theater before."

"How do you know?" I asked. "There must be three hundred people in here."

"I have ESP," he said. "Now go back to your own movie."

"This is our movie," Nate said. "We just came late. That's why you didn't see us before."

"Yeah? Where are your ticket stubs?"

All the stubs have the number of the theater on them, so you can't get into, say, Ten if your ticket says Five.

"We lost them," I said.

"When you find them you can come in."

He opened the door and practically pushed us out.

Nate glared at me as I stood there, helpless, wondering if Darlene had managed to sneak in and sit next to Warren, wondering if at this very minute she was squealing and clutching at him and hiding her gorgeous face in his satin team jacket.

"You want to try for *Young Cutthroats?*"
I said glumly.

"How are we going to get into the 'R' movie if they won't even let us into the 'PG' movie?" Nate demanded.

"I don't know. I don't care. Let's just cut out."

"Oh, no. We paid good money for a movie, and I want to see a movie."

"You didn't pay," I said. "*I* paid. And you know why. Come on, Nate. I feel bad enough without sitting through another hour of toe dancing."

"We came to see a movie and I'm going to see a movie," Nate insisted. He had a sort of crazy gleam in his eye again, and I couldn't figure out why he was being so stubborn, especially since I'd had to strong-arm him into *Toujours Jeté* in the first place.

I guessed he was just paying me back. And I didn't want to get my other biceps punched. So we trudged back to Theater Five and as we stumbled down the aisle in the dark, Nate suddenly pushed me sideways into a seat behind a girl with a big frizzy mop of hair.

"Oof," I grunted and the girl turned around and said, delightedly, "Oh, hi, Hobie! I thought you didn't see me before."

And Nate cackled softly to himself while G. G. Graffman wiggled past my knees and plopped into the seat next to me.

"Now," Nate whispered, "we're even."

"I didn't know you liked ballet, Hobie," G. G. whispered. She had her head right next to mine, so I could hear her.

"I hate ballet." I leaned sideways, shifting in my seat before her cheek could touch my face.

"Oh," she said. Then, "Ohhh," as if she suddenly understood something.

I stared straight ahead for a few minutes, watching the screen. A woman twirled on her toes as a long red scarf unwound from her waist. A guy in tights and a satin jacket held onto one end, gathering up the scarf. Then she began twirling the other way, winding the scarf around herself again. The whole thing seemed pretty pointless.

"Would you like a Bon Bon?" G. G. held out the box.

"Thanks." I took a Bon Bon and wondered if I had just made a fatal error. Bon Bons are pretty expensive. If I ate one, did it mean I owed her anything?

I tried to watch the movie. But every once in a while I could see G. G. from the corner of my eye, sneaking glances at me. I kept shifting around in my seat, getting more and more uncomfortable. I probably looked like I had to go to the bathroom.

Finally the movie ended. I nearly leaped out of my seat and tried to push past Nate to get to the aisle. Nate had his legs stretched across the seat in front of him and didn't seem in any big hurry to leave.

"Move it, Nate."

"What's your rush?" He grinned. Lazily he lifted one foot off the back of the seat. I could feel G. G.'s hot breath on the back of my neck.

She tapped me on the shoulder. "Hobie? You want a ride home? My mother's picking me up."

"No. Nate's mother is coming for us."

"Oh." She sounded disappointed.

Nate lifted his other foot off the seat and stood up. "You can come with us," he said, looking right past me to G. G. "My mother won't mind."

"Oh, thanks!" G. G. crowed.

I gave him a look that would have made King Kong's fur stand on end. He smiled calmly and led the way out of the movies to the telephone booths in the middle of the mall.

G. sat next to me in the back seat of Mrs. Kramer's Datsun. I kept all the way over to my side, near the window, and wished G. G. would have the good sense to keep all the way over to her side. But she didn't. She kept edging closer and closer to me, till my only escape route was the sun roof.

Mrs. Kramer made a sharp right. I was thrown sideways, right against the back corner of the car. G. G. was thrown sideways, right against me.

"Ooops." She clutched at my jacket, maybe trying to get her balance. She smelled of chocolate and artificially buttered popcorn. I grabbed at her hands, trying to get them unclutched from my jacket. Mrs. Kramer made a sharp left.

We swung to the left and suddenly—I don't know how it happened—our hands were clasped together and my nose was flattened against G. G.'s cheek and I couldn't straighten up because her fingers were like steel clamps around mine.

"Oh, *Hobie*," she murmured.

In sheer panic I prepared to elbow her in the gut and launch myself out the sun roof, but just then the car jerked to a stop and I realized we were in front of my house.

G. G. let go of my hands. I yanked the back door open and exploded out of the car like I was shot from a cannon.

I didn't begin to relax until I was shut in my room with the lights off.

And even then I kept wanting to shove a chair under the doorknob.

I was shooting layups in the driveway the next morning when I heard Nate's voice.

"There he goes, straight for the hoop, eluding the pressing two-on-one defense—"

I whirled around. "Get off my property."

"The sidewalk is county property," Nate said. "Act your age, Hobe."

"*Me? Me* act my age? Get out of here."

"Aw come on, Horrible Hobe. Just consider us even."

"We were even when you dragged me back into the ballet movie and shoved me into G. G. After that ride home, I owe you one."

"Listen, that's what I came to talk to you about. You know what you were thinking about G. G.? That book she bought? And how you might be the guy she wanted to make crazy?"

"Yeah?"

"I think you were right."

I leaned against the garage door and tried to keep my eyeballs from turning up inside my lids.

"I knew it," I said. "I *knew* it. How far has she gotten in the book?"

"I don't know. She didn't say anything about the book. But she asked me if I thought you liked her."

I narrowed my eyes and glared at him, like Mac Detroit faced Don Vitello Tonnato in *Sicilian Slay Ride.* "You told her that I hated the mere sight of her, didn't you? That the thought of going out with her was enough to make me sign up with the Foreign Legion for the next twenty years? You told her something like that, right?"

"Well . . . not exactly."

"Then what, exactly?" I prepared to heave the basketball at his head and race off to the nearest Foreign Legion recruiting office.

"I said I didn't know."

"You didn't *know?*" I heaved the basketball at his head. "What do you mean, you didn't know? I *told* you—"

"You told me she didn't really make you sick," Nate said. "So I figured you weren't sure about how you felt."

"I told you I didn't want to go out with a Marine Biologist!"

"Well, she's not a Marine Biologist yet," Nate said sarcastically. "She could always change her mind and become the waitress of your dreams."

"You know something, Nate? At the rate you're going, it'll take me ten years to get even." I slammed my hand against the garage door and wished it was Nate's face.

"Maybe eleven," Nate said nervously. "Look who's coming."

I turned around.

Down the street, riding like the wind and heading toward my house like a killer tornado, was G. G. Graffman on her trusty bike.

"I guess I'd better get on home," Nate said. "See you, Hobe."

"This is all your fault!" I yelled as G. G. sped toward

us. "And you're going to walk off and leave me here alone with—"

G. G. whizzed past us, past my house and up to the corner, where she made a swooping left at the cross street.

"What was that all about?" Nate said.

"Maybe she was going somewhere and this street happened to be on the way?" I cheered up a little.

Or maybe it was just her first lap," Nate said. "Listen, it's not my fault. You're the one who swept her off her sneakers with your dazzling charm." He eyed me critically. "I can't see it myself," he added, "but there's no accounting for—"

"Here she comes again. You stay right where you are."

G. G. was heading back down the street, her knees pumping like pistons.

"She's going to wear her little toes to a nub," Nate said. He whipped his head around as she hurtled past us again, going back the way she'd originally come. "Lap two, cycle fans, and aiming for a new record!"

"What on earth is she doing?" I said. "And why is she doing it to *me?*"

"Hey, Hobe, this is getting a little repetitive. And if she ever does put her brakes on, I don't want to be here. It'll be embarrassing for her if you have to fight off her amorous advances in front of me. That's a real personal thing between a guy and a girl."

"I don't want to be around either," I said. "I'm going inside."

"See you later," Nate said. "And I still don't know what's so repulsive about G. G."

"Then *you* go with her."

"I'm not the one she wants to drive crazy," Nate said. He stuck his hands in his pockets and walked off down the street.

CRASH

SQUEAL OF RUBBER, A FEMALE SHRIEK, A CLASH OF METAL AND THEN A HOWL OF PAIN

My hand was on the doorknob when I heard a squeal of rubber, a female shriek, a clash of metal, and then a howl of pain.

Even as I turned around I told myself I shouldn't look. I should go right in the house and draw all the blinds and shove a chair under my doorknob. Because it was certainly G. G. and she had probably broken both legs and would have to be carried into my house, where she would spend six weeks with her legs in casts and nothing to do but read *How to Make Men Crazy,* and—

Sure enough, G. G. Graffman was sprawled halfway on the lawn, halfway in our driveway, tangled up in her bike. The back wheel was still spinning and G. G. was moaning softly.

Reluctantly I walked down the lawn to the scene of the accident and bent down. "Are you okay?"

"I think my shoulder—maybe my elbow too," she whimpered. "Might be broken. Am I bleeding?"

So it wasn't her legs. So it was her elbow and shoulder. She'd still spend the next six weeks in our house in traction, I thought gloomily.

I didn't see any blood, so I said, "Do you think you can stand up?" If she could stand up, she could make it to a hospital.

She grunted. "Not till you get the bike off me."

Carefully I gripped the handlebars, grabbed the seat, and lifted the bike away from G. G. I pushed it onto the grass. "Can you get up now?"

"I think so. If you'll just pull me up *very gently*." She held out her hand.

This is all a plot, I thought, to get me to hold her hand. But anything to get her on her feet and out of my life.

I took her hand and pulled.

"Gently!" she screamed. She made it to her knees, then stood up, shakily.

"Ohh, Hobie," she groaned. She sagged against me. I panicked and grabbed her shoulders to push her away.

"Ouch! Hobie, that hurts!"

I let go of her shoulders and she sagged right back into me again. A point on the collar of her down vest poked me in the nose.

A nine-year-old neighbor who I'd always thought was a good kid zipped by on a skateboard. "Hobie's got a girlfriend, Hobie's got a girlfriend!"

G. G. was still using my chest as a leaning post and my shoulder as a pillow. It looked like we were going to be standing there forever, and I began to plan in what order I wanted to terminate people. Nate first, or G. G.?

"Do you, Hobie?" G. G. asked. She finally managed to tear herself away from me.

I quickly backed away before she could lean on me again. "Do I what?"

G. G. didn't look at me, but concentrated on the shoulder she was gently rubbing. "Have a girlfriend?"

Now what? Before the panic could set in again I asked myself what Mac Detroit would do in a situation like this. Simple. He'd either grab her and kiss her lips which were like ripe fruit or push her out of his hotel room with a terse but pithy putdown, such as, "Sorry, Sweetheart, I've got other flounders to fillet."

Neither option was viable, since the first was out of the question and the second required a hotel room to push G. G. out of. I began to wonder if Mac Detroit had ever faced a really dangerous situation like this one, or if he merely spent his days flirting with death.

"Listen, G. G., that was a pretty bad fall you had. You'd better get right home and lie down." I didn't care whether she went to bed or hung from the dining room chandelier, as long as she did it at her house. "And be careful!"

"I was being careful," she said. "I was just trying to do a wheelie."

"A *wheelie?* At your age?" I didn't want to prolong the conversation, but I really was surprised—even if G. G. was immature. At least I'd gotten her mind off my love life and onto her bike. Now if I could only get G. G. onto her bike . . .

"I know, I know. It was stupid. But it wasn't all my fault. I think you have a crack in your driveway. And I only did it to—I mean—I haven't tried a wheelie in years. I just wanted—well, you *did* notice me."

I hadn't gotten her mind off me at all. But I felt a little less nervous; it really was just a matter of saying, "Scram, Sweetheart, I have other chickens to fricassee," and that would be that.

"All right," I said gruffly. "I noticed you. The whole block noticed you. Now, scram, Sweetheart, I have other chickens to fricassee."

She stared at me, her eyes all round and her mouth slightly open. She knew a brush-off when she heard one, I thought, elated. Maybe old Mac Detroit really does have all the answers!

"Oh, Hobie . . . ," she sighed.

"Whaaat?" I snarled. "What now?"

"Hobie . . . you called me sweetheart!"

Ellen Conford as a teenager

Finding Myself

Ellen Conford

When I was in junior high school, I was convinced that there was a secret to being popular. The kids everyone admired—the ones who had tons of friends, who went to all the school dances, who were always elected class officers—knew something that I didn't about how to make people like you.

I never had the nerve to ask any of these kids what the secret was. In fact, I was too shy to speak to them at all.

Like the Extremely Shy Person in "What Do I Do Now?," I needed help. So I pored through teen magazines, advice columns and books looking for a magic formula that would turn me into the Terrific Teen I wanted to be.

But all the articles, all the books, all the advice columns said the same things. "Show other people that you are interested in them. Be yourself. *Smile!*"

What kind of advice was that? If you're too timid to start conversations with people, how can you show them you're interested in them? As for being myself—if I were satisfied with myself, I wouldn't be

BY ELLEN CONFORD

reading all this stuff about how to be different.

I *did* know how to smile—but what did I have to smile about?

When I fell in love—which I did approximately every three weeks—I studied harder: "How to Talk to the Opposite Sex," "How to Get Along with Boys," and "A Teenager's Guide to Dating." (Not that I needed a guide to dating—I didn't have any dates.)

What did all these experts tell me? "If you like someone, let him know."

Were they kidding? I could never have done what G. G. Graffman does in "Alias Mac Detroit." I could never have been so open about liking a boy.

So when I fell in love with someone, what I did mainly was walk my dog past his house. A lot. Hoping that HE would come out and mow the lawn. Or wash the car. Or yell, "Hi, Ellen!" as I strolled casually by.

It never worked. I would get discouraged, and my cocker spaniel would get sore feet and hide from me every time I waved her leash.

Gradually I guess I got tired of trying to think up ways to make people like me. Instead, I began to concentrate on the things I liked to do.

I loved to read and write, so I joined the school newspaper and humor magazine. I liked acting (where I didn't have to be myself!), so I joined the drama club. I liked jazz music, and I joined the jazz club.

In those groups I met people who liked to read, liked to write, liked to act, and liked to listen to music. It was easy to talk to them—there was no secret to it at all. We were interested in the same things, and we worked on projects together that we all enjoyed.

I didn't change my personality to try and make people like me. I just discovered the things I loved to do and did them.

I found plenty of friends, once I found myself.

Thinking About It

Hobie says, "Drastic times call for drastic measures." Which character are you in this story? Would you be a new character? What would you do and why?

Ellen Conford is always looking for new ideas for her next book. What would you like her to write about? Why would your ideas make a good Conford story?

G. G. is working her way through her book, *How to Make Men Crazy*. Do you think it's working so far? What do you think G. G. has in mind next?

Another Book About Friends

Hobie isn't the only one with "friend problems." In *The Genuine, Ingenious, Thrift Shop Genie, Clarissa Mae Bean and Me* by Beverly Keller, Marcie's friendship with Clarissa has made Marcie an outcast with her "friends." Marcie learns surprising lessons about relationships.

THE SIDEWALK RACER
or On the Skateboard
by Lillian Morrison

Skimming
an asphalt sea
I swerve, I curve, I
sway; I speed to whirring
sound an inch above the
ground; I'm the sailor
and the sail, I'm the
driver and the wheel
I'm the one and only
single engine
human auto
mobile.

I'LL WALK THE TIGHTROPE
by Margaret Danner

I'll walk the tightrope that's been stretched for me,

and though a wrinkled forehead, perplexed why,

will accompany me, I'll delicately

step along. For if I stop to sigh

at the earth-propped stride

of others, I will fall. I must balance high

without a parasol to tide

a faltering step, without a net below,

without a balance stick to guide.

THE FULLER BRUSH MAN

DONALD LEANED INTO the car trunk to find the box holding the giveaways. He had to pay for each letter opener, shoehorn, and vegetable brush, money out of his own commission, but it was worth it. Why else would people listen to his sales spiel if it wasn't because they felt indebted the second they reached for a sample?

What a mess, he thought, getting grease on his hand. Ever since Mom stopped driving. Ever since she . . . Well, there was no use dwelling on that. When he had time he'd try to get rid of some of the junk. He dropped a dozen plastic shoehorns into his sample case, snapped the lock, and glanced at his watch.

Man, he was hungry. He'd been working steadily since right after school, four hours. All he'd eaten was a doughnut left in the breadbox at home, running out the door with Ava calling after him to get a glass of milk first.

by Gloria D. Miklowitz

He'd sold enough brushes to call it quits for the day, but maybe he'd work another hour. If he went home now, even though it would mean a real meal, not McDonald's, Ava would be there. Their newest house-keeper, she'd sit there at the kitchen table, arms folded, watching him, and she'd go into her usual song and dance.

"Go in to your mother. Just for a minute. Say hello. Say *some*thing."

"Later."

"*Now*. She'll be asleep later."

"Why? She can't talk. She probably doesn't even know who I am. What difference does it make?"

"Donnie, Donnie. You love her. I know you do. Do it for you, if not for her."

"Leave me alone."

He'd get this picture in his head of Mom, the way she had become lately. Bloated face, dull eyes that fol-lowed him without seeming to see, a stomach as if she was pregnant. And her arms skinny, all bones. *Why? How could she do that to him, to them?*

No. He'd just get a bite nearby and go home later. He could maybe make five more sales. More money for the college fund. And with what Dad was putting out in medical bills and nursing care, every cent counted.

He crossed the street and was nearly knocked down by a kid on a two-wheeler, shooting out of a driveway, wobbling his way down the road. When had *he* learned to ride a bike? Eight, nine years ago? Yes. In the Apperson Street schoolyard, late afternoons. He could hear the crickets chirping even now, and for a second he felt the same surge of fear and exultation he'd felt then gripping the handlebars.

"I can't! I can't! I'm falling! Mom, Mom! Help me!"

"You can! You can! Keep going! That's right! You're doing it!"

Running alongside, face sweating and flushed, red hair flying about her eyes and cheeks, she was laughing with joy. And when he finally managed to stop she threw her arms around him and cried, "See? You did it! I knew you could!"

He swallowed a lump in his throat and marched briskly up the walk to the door of a small, wooden house. He rang the bell and waited, peering through the screen door into a living room with a worn couch, a TV flickering against one wall, and a small child sitting in front of it.

"If you don't behave, you'll have to watch TV," his mother would say when he was that age, as if watching TV was punishment. Maybe that's why he hardly watched even now.

When *he* was little, this was the time of day he loved most. Right after supper and before bedtime. He'd climb up on the couch to sit beside Mom. Bonnie would take her place on Mom's other side and for a half hour it was "weed books" time.

He felt an overwhelming hunger for those times, for Mom's arm around him and her warm voice reading. He wiped a hand across his eyes as a woman, holding a baby, came to the door.

"Fuller brush man! Good evening, missus. Would you like a sample?" Donald held out a brush, a letter opener, and a shoehorn. With but a second's hesitation the woman unlatched the door and stepped forward, eyeing the samples greedily. She took the brush.

"Good choice," Donald said. "They're great for scrubbing vegetables. Now, would you like to see our specials?" He held the catalog open to the specials page, but the light was fading.

"I don't need any . . ."

"Then maybe you'd like to try our new tile-cleaning foam. See?" He plucked a can from his case and showed

her the cap with its stiff bristles for the "hard-to-clean places between the tiles."

"I have Formica."

"Sally? Sally? Who the devil is that?"

"Just a brush salesman, honey!"

"Well, tell him you don't need any!"

The woman gave him a sheepish grin, backed away, and said, "Sorry." She closed the screen door and latched it again.

He used to take rejection hard, getting a pain in his stomach that grew with each door shut in his face, each disgusted "Don't bother me." He still withdrew inside when people turned him away, although he wouldn't show it now, keeping his voice pleasant and a smile on his face. If anyone asked, he'd say he hated the job even though he was learning a lot about human nature and keeping books, and it did pay well.

"Sell door to door?" his mother had asked when he first proposed the idea. "Absolutely not!"

"Why not? I could save what I make for college!"

"No!"

"Why? That's not fair!"

"Because." He watched her struggle to find words for what she hadn't thought out. "Because it's not safe, knocking on strange people's doors. The world is full of crazies. Because I don't want you to have to get doors slammed in your face. Because it will be summer soon and too hot to work outdoors. If you want a job, find one where it's air-conditioned."

"Let him try," Dad said. "One day of it and he'll quit."

"*Please*, Mom?"

"Oh, all right," she conceded, but only because that morning he'd accused her of still treating him like a baby. "But only to try it. *One* day!"

It was three months now. She must have been sick even then, because after that first day when he'd come home triumphant with having made fifty-four dollars in only six hours, he didn't hear anything more about quitting. It was about then that she went into the hospital for the first time and his whole life began to change.

When he finished another block, he circled back to the car, a dog barking at his heels. One of the hazards of selling things in strange neighborhoods was the dogs. He found that if he stood his ground and shouted "No," most dogs would go through their ferocious act and run off when they figured they'd done their duty.

In the dim light of the car he looked over his orders and decided to drive down to the boulevard for something to eat. Maybe he'd phone Shannon afterwards, drop by for a few minutes before going home. He started the engine, turned on the headlights, and drove down the hill.

"How's your Mom?" Shannon asked when he reached her from the phone in the parking lot. There was so much traffic noise he had to press the receiver tight against his ear.

"What are you doing?" he asked in response. "I can be by in ten minutes. We could go for a walk."

"When are you going to talk about it?" Shannon asked. "Bonnie says she's worse. It's awful how you're acting. It's not her fault."

For a second he considered not answering at all, but finally he said, "Stop bugging me. Everyone's after me about it. It's *my* mom. It's my business. If that's all you want to talk about, forget it."

"But, Donnie! You can't put it off much longer."

He hung up without answering and ran back to the car.

Slamming the door, he slumped in the driver's seat and stared out at the ribbon of lights on the freeway. If he let himself think about what Shannon said, he'd just start blubbering like a baby. Better to work. He'd get at the orders for the week. They were due to be toted up and recorded on the big order sheet by tomorrow. Usually he'd work on it at home, spreading the papers out on his desk and marking how many of this or that he'd sold that week. But if he went home now, they'd *all* be there: Dad, Bonnie, and Ava. All accusing. Bonnie with her *Please, Donnie*'s. Ava with her *Why don't you*'s. And Dad with his sad silence, worse than words.

But worst of all was knowing that Mom lay in the next room wasting away, dying, not even fighting anymore. He felt that if he was forced to go in there, all he'd do is scream at her. "Don't you care? Try! You always told us never to give up! You're not trying!" And he'd want to strike out at her. Well, maybe not at her, but at something!

There wasn't a moment in the day that he didn't think about her. It was as if they were joined by an invisible wire and he felt everything she did. And he felt now that she was slipping away. He couldn't stop it. He couldn't do a thing about it. There was nothing to say, nothing! Everything he thought of saying sounded false or stupid.

Well, all right! If that's what he had to do, he'd do it. He'd *go* home. He'd go into her room. He'd look at that woman who was and wasn't his mother anymore and he'd say *something*. Whatever came into his head, no matter how mean or dumb. *All right!* If that's what they all wanted, that's what he'd do.

He turned the key in the ignition and gunned the car out of the parking lot and into the street. He drove above the speed limit, mouth clenched in a tight line, totally intent on the road, mind empty except for the determination to get home fast.

He parked the car in the drive and ran into the house. Suddenly he was terribly afraid. What if it was too late? He almost felt in his gut that he'd waited too long.

"Donnie?" Dad called from the family room. "That you?"

He made some kind of guttural response and ran past the room, not even nodding. He had a fleeting sense that Dad was there reading the paper, that Bonnie was doing homework. His heart hammered loudly in his ears. An electrical pulse ran down his arms to his legs as he reached his mother's bedroom door and put a hand on the knob.

And then he stopped. For a long moment he stood waiting for his legs to quit trembling, for his heart to slow down. And then he closed his eyes, took a deep breath, and straightened his shoulders. Fixing a smile on his face, he knocked. "Fuller brush man!" he called, lightly opening the door.

THINKING ABOUT IT

Both Ava and Bonnie try to convince Donnie to visit his ill mother. What would you, as Donnie's friend, say to him to help him through this situation?

If you were writing this story, would you make Donnie a nicer character or a worse character or the same? How would Ava, Bonnie, and Donnie's father act toward him? Explain.

The story ends when Donnie knocks on his mother's door and calls "Fuller brush man!" What does he say to his mother? What does his mother say to him? Explain why you think so.

RULES
OF THE
GAME

I WAS SIX WHEN my mother taught me the art of invisible strength. It was a strategy for winning arguments, respect from others, and eventually, though neither of us knew it at the time, chess games.

"Bite back your tongue," scolded my mother when I cried loudly, yanking her hand toward the store that sold bags of salted plums. At home, she said, "Wise guy, he not go against wind. In Chinese we say, Come from South, blow with wind—poom!—North will follow. Strongest wind cannot be seen."

The next week I bit back my tongue as we entered the store with the forbidden candies. When my mother finished her shopping, she quietly plucked a small bag of plums from the rack and put it on the counter with the rest of the items.

by Amy Tan

My mother imparted her daily truths so she could help my older brothers and me rise above our circumstances. We lived in San Francisco's Chinatown. Like most of the other Chinese children who played in the back alleys of restaurants and curio shops, I didn't think we were poor. My bowl was always full, three five-course meals every day, beginning with a soup full of mysterious things I didn't want to know the names of.

We lived on Waverly Place, in a warm, clean, two-bedroom flat that sat above a small Chinese bakery specializing in steamed pastries and dim sum. In the early morning, when the alley was still quiet, I could smell fragrant red beans as they were cooked down to a pasty sweetness. By daybreak, our flat was heavy with the odor of fried sesame balls and sweet curried chicken crescents. From my bed, I would listen as my father got ready for work, then locked the door behind him, one-two-three clicks.

At the end of our two-block alley was a small sandlot playground with swings and slides well-shined down the middle with use. The play area was bordered by wood-slat benches where old-country people sat cracking roasted watermelon seeds with their golden teeth and scattering the husks to an impatient gathering of gurgling pigeons. The best playground, however, was the dark alley itself. It was crammed with daily mysteries and adventures. My brothers and I would peer into the medicinal herb shop, watching old Li dole out onto a stiff sheet of white paper the right amount of insect shells, saffron-colored seeds, and pungent leaves for his ailing customers. It was said that he once cured a woman dying of an ancestral curse that had eluded the best of American doctors. Next to the pharmacy was a printer who specialized in gold-embossed wedding invitations and festive red banners.

Farther down the street was Ping Yuen Fish Market. The front window displayed a tank crowded with doomed fish and turtles struggling to gain footing on the slimy green-tiled sides. A handwritten sign informed tourists, "Within this store, is all for food, not for pet." Inside, the butchers with their bloodstained white smocks deftly gutted the fish while customers cried out their orders and shouted, "Give me your freshest," to which the butchers always protested, "All are freshest." On less crowded market days, we would inspect the crates of live frogs and crabs which we were warned not to poke, boxes of dried cuttlefish, and row upon row of iced prawns, squid, and slippery fish. The sanddabs made me shiver each time; their eyes lay on one flattened side and reminded me of my mother's story of a careless girl who ran into a crowded street and was crushed by a cab. "Was smash flat," reported my mother.

At the corner of the alley was Hong Sing's, a four-table café with a recessed stairwell in front that led to a door marked "Tradesmen." My brothers and I believed the bad people emerged from this door at night. Tourists never went to Hong Sing's, since the menu was printed only in Chinese. A Caucasian man with a big camera once posed me and my playmates in front of the restaurant. He had us move to the side of the picture window so the photo would capture the roasted duck with its head dangling from a juice-covered rope. After he took the picture, I told him he should go into Hong Sing's and eat dinner. When he smiled and asked me what they served, I shouted, "Guts and duck's feet and octopus gizzards!" Then I ran off with my friends, shrieking with laughter as we scampered across the alley and hid in the entryway grotto of the China Gem Company, my heart pounding with hope that he would chase us.

My mother named me after the street that we lived on: Waverly Place Jong, my official name for important American documents. But my family called me Meimei, "Little Sister." I was the youngest, the only daughter. Each morning before school, my mother would twist and yank on my thick black hair until she had formed two tightly wound pigtails. One day, as she struggled to weave a hard-toothed comb through my disobedient hair, I had a sly thought.

I asked her, "Ma, what is Chinese torture?" My mother shook her head. A bobby pin was wedged between her lips. She wetted her palm and smoothed the hair above my ear, then pushed the pin in so that it nicked sharply against my scalp.

"Who say this word?" she asked without a trace of knowing how wicked I was being. I shrugged my shoulders and said, "Some boy in my class said Chinese people do Chinese torture."

"Chinese people do many things," she said simply. "Chinese people do business, do medicine, do painting. Not lazy like American people. We do torture. Best torture."

My older brother Vincent was the one who actually got the chess set. We had gone to the annual Christmas party held at the First Chinese Baptist Church at the end of the alley. The missionary ladies had put together a Santa bag of gifts donated by members of another church. None of the gifts had names on them. There were separate sacks for boys and girls of different ages.

One of the Chinese parishioners had donned a Santa

Claus costume and a stiff paper beard with cotton balls glued to it. I think the only children who thought he was the real thing were too young to know that Santa Claus was not Chinese. When my turn came up, the Santa man asked me how old I was. I thought it was a trick question; I was seven according to the American formula and eight by the Chinese calendar. I said I was born on March 17, 1951. That seemed to satisfy him. He then solemnly asked if I had been a very, very good girl this year and did I believe in Jesus Christ and obey my parents. I knew the only answer to that. I nodded back with equal solemnity.

Having watched the other children opening their gifts, I already knew that the big gifts were not necessarily the nicest ones. One girl my age got a large coloring book of biblical characters, while a less greedy girl who selected a smaller box received a glass vial of lavender toilet water. The sound of the box was also important. A ten-year-old boy had chosen a box that jangled when he shook it. It was a tin globe of the world with a slit for inserting money. He must have thought it was full of dimes and nickels, because when he saw that it had just ten pennies, his face fell with such undisguised disappointment that his mother slapped the side of his head and led him out of the church hall, apologizing to the crowd for her son who had such bad manners he couldn't appreciate such a fine gift.

As I peered into the sack, I quickly fingered the remaining presents, testing their weight, imagining what they contained. I chose a heavy, compact one that was wrapped in shiny silver foil and a red satin ribbon. It was a twelve-pack of Life Savers and I spent the rest of the party arranging and rearranging the candy tubes in the order of my favorites. My brother Winston chose wisely as well. His present turned out to be a box of intricate plastic parts; the instructions on the box proclaimed that when they were properly assembled he would have an authentic miniature replica of a World War II submarine.

Vincent got the chess set, which would have been a very decent present to get at a church Christmas party, except it was obviously used and, as we discovered later, it was missing a black pawn and a white knight. My mother graciously thanked the unknown benefactor, saying, "Too good. Cost too much." At which point, an old lady with fine white, wispy hair nodded toward our family and said with a whistling whisper, "Merry, merry Christmas."

When we got home, my mother told Vincent to throw the chess set away. "She not want it. We not want it," she said, tossing her head stiffly to the side with a tight, proud smile. My brothers had deaf ears. They were already lining up the chess pieces and reading from the dog-eared instruction book.

I watched Vincent and Winston play during Christmas week. The chess board seemed to hold elaborate secrets waiting to be untangled. The chessmen were more powerful than Old Li's magic herbs that cured ancestral curses. And my brothers wore such serious faces that I was sure something was at stake that was greater than avoiding the tradesmen's door to Hong Sing's.

"Let me! Let me!" I begged between games when one brother or the other would sit back with a deep sigh of relief and victory, the other annoyed, unable to let go of the outcome. Vincent at first refused to let me play, but when I offered my Life Savers as replacements for the buttons that filled in for the missing pieces, he relented. He chose the flavors: wild cherry for the black pawn and peppermint for the white knight. Winner could eat both.

As our mother sprinkled flour and rolled out small doughy circles for the steamed dumplings that would be our dinner that night, Vincent explained the rules, pointing to each piece. "You have sixteen pieces and so do I. One king and queen, two bishops, two knights, two castles, and eight pawns. The pawns can only move forward one step, except on the first move. Then they can move two. But they can only take men by moving crossways like this, except in the beginning, when you can move ahead and take another pawn."

"Why?" I asked as I moved my pawn. "Why can't they move more steps?"

"Because they're pawns," he said.

"But why do they go crossways to take other men? Why aren't there any women and children?"

"Why is the sky blue? Why must you always ask stupid questions?" asked Vincent. "This is a game. These are the rules. I didn't make them up. See. Here. In the book." He jabbed a page with a pawn in his hand. "Pawn. P-A-W-N. Pawn. Read it yourself."

My mother patted the flour off her hands. "Let me see book," she said quietly. She scanned the pages quickly, not reading the foreign English symbols, seeming to search deliberately for nothing in particular.

"This American rules," she concluded at last. "Every time people come out from foreign country, must know rules. You not know, judge say, Too bad, go back. They not telling you why so you can use their way go forward. They say, Don't know why, you find out yourself. But they knowing all the time. Better you take it, find out why yourself." She tossed her head back with a satisfied smile.

I found out about all the whys later. I read the rules and looked up all the big words in a dictionary. I borrowed books from the Chinatown library. I studied each chess piece, trying to absorb the power each contained.

I learned about opening moves and why it's important to control the center early on; the shortest distance between two points is straight down the middle. I learned about the middle game and why tactics between two adversaries are like clashing ideas; the one who plays better has the clearest plans for both attacking and getting out of traps. I learned why it is essential in the endgame to have foresight, a mathematical understanding of all possible moves, and patience; all weaknesses and advantages become evident to a strong adversary and are obscured to a tiring opponent. I discovered that for the whole game one must gather invisible strengths and see the endgame before the game begins.

I also found out why I should never reveal "why" to others. A little knowledge withheld is a great advantage one should store for future use. That is the power of chess. It is a game of secrets in which one must show and never tell.

I loved the secrets I found within the sixty-four black and white squares. I carefully drew a handmade chessboard and pinned it to the wall next to my bed, where at night I would stare for hours at imaginary battles. Soon I no longer lost any games or Life Savers, but I lost my adversaries. Winston and Vincent decided they were more interested in roaming the streets after school in their Hopalong Cassidy cowboy hats.[1]

---

[1]Hopalong Cassidy was once a popular cowboy character in the movies and on television who always wore a large black cowboy hat.

On a cold spring afternoon, while walking home from school, I detoured through the playground at the end of our alley. I saw a group of old men, two seated across a folding table playing a game of chess, others smoking pipes, eating peanuts, and watching. I ran home and grabbed Vincent's chess set, which was bound in a cardboard box with rubber bands. I also carefully selected two prized rolls of Life Savers. I came back to the park and approached a man who was observing the game.

"Want to play?" I asked him. His face widened with surprise and he grinned as he looked at the box under my arm.

"Little sister, been a long time since I play with dolls," he said, smiling benevolently. I quickly put the box down next to him on the bench and displayed my retort.

Lau Po, as he allowed me to call him, turned out to be a much better player than my brothers. I lost many games and many Life Savers. But over the weeks, with each diminishing roll of candies, I added new secrets. Lau Po gave me the names. The Double Attack from the East and West Shores. Throwing Stones on the Drowning Man. The Sudden Meeting of the Clan. The Surprise from the Sleeping Guard. The Humble Servant Who Kills the King. Sand in the Eyes of Advancing Forces. A Double Killing Without Blood.

There were also the fine points of chess etiquette. Keep captured men in neat rows, as well-tended prisoners. Never announce "Check" with vanity, lest someone with an unseen sword slit your throat. Never hurl pieces into the sandbox after you have lost a game, because then you must find them again, by yourself, after apologizing to all around you. By the end of the summer, Lau Po had taught me all he knew, and I had become a better chess player.

A small weekend crowd of Chinese people and tourists would gather as I played and defeated my opponents one by one. My mother would join the crowds during these outdoor exhibition games. She sat proudly on the bench, telling my admirers with proper Chinese humility, "Is luck."

A man who watched me play in the park suggested that my mother allow me to play in local chess tournaments. My mother smiled graciously, an answer that meant nothing. I desperately wanted to go, but I bit back my tongue. I knew she would not let me play among strangers. So as we walked home I said in a small voice that I didn't want to play in the local tournament. They would have American rules. If I lost, I would bring shame on my family.

"Is shame you fall down nobody push you," said my mother.

During my first tournament, my mother sat with me in the front row as I waited for my turn. I frequently bounced my legs to unstick them from the cold metal seat of the folding chair. When my name was called, I leapt up. My mother unwrapped something in her lap. It was her *chang,* a small tablet of red jade which held the sun's fire. "Is luck," she whispered, and tucked it into my dress pocket. I turned to my opponent, a fifteen-year-old boy from Oakland. He looked at me, wrinkling his nose.

As I began to play, the boy disappeared, the color ran out of the room, and I saw only my white pieces and his black ones waiting on the other side. A light wind began blowing past my ears. It whispered secrets only I could hear.

"Blow from the South," it murmured. "The wind leaves no trail." I saw a clear path, the traps to avoid. The crowd rustled. "Shhh! Shhh!" said the corners of the room. The wind blew stronger. "Throw sand from the East to distract him." The knight came forward ready for the sacrifice. The wind hissed, louder and louder. "Blow, blow, blow. He cannot see. He is blind now. Make him lean away from the wind so he is easier to knock down."

"Check," I said, as the wind roared with laughter. The wind died down to little puffs, my own breath.

My mother placed my first trophy next to a new plastic chess set that the neighborhood Tao society had given to me. As she wiped each piece with a soft cloth, she said, "Next time win more, lose less."

"Ma, it's not how many pieces you lose," I said. "Sometimes you need to lose pieces to get ahead."

"Better to lose less, see if you really need."

At the next tournament, I won again, but it was my mother who wore the triumphant grin.

"Lost eight piece this time. Last time was eleven. What I tell you? Better off lose less!" I was annoyed, but I couldn't say anything.

I attended more tournaments, each one farther away from home. I won all games, in all divisions. The Chinese bakery downstairs from our flat displayed my growing collection of trophies in its window, amidst the dust-covered cakes that were never picked up. The day after I won an important regional tournament, the window encased a fresh sheet cake with whipped-cream frosting and red script saying, "Congratulations, Waverly Jong, Chinatown Chess Champion." Soon after that, a flower shop, headstone engraver, and funeral parlor offered to sponsor me in national tournaments. That's when my mother decided I no longer had to do the dishes. Winston and Vincent had to do my chores.

"Why does she get to play and we do all the work," complained Vincent.

"Is new American rules," said my mother. "Meimei play, squeeze all her brains out for win chess. You play, worth squeeze towel."

By my ninth birthday, I was a national chess champion. I was still some 429 points away from grand-master status, but I was touted as the Great American Hope, a child prodigy and a girl to boot. They ran a photo of me in *Life* magazine next to a quote in which Bobby Fischer said, "There will never be a woman grand master." "Your move, Bobby," said the caption.

The day they took the magazine picture I wore neatly plaited braids clipped with plastic barrettes trimmed with rhinestones. I was playing in a large high school auditorium that echoed with phlegmy coughs and the squeaky rubber knobs of chair legs sliding across freshly waxed wooden floors. Seated across from me was an American man, about the same age as Lau Po, maybe fifty. I remember that his sweaty brow seemed to weep at my every move. He wore a dark, malodorous suit. One of his pockets was stuffed with a great white kerchief on which he wiped his palm before sweeping his hand over the chosen chess piece with great flourish.

In my crisp pink-and-white dress with scratchy lace at the neck, one of two my mother had sewn for these special occasions, I would clasp my hands under my chin, the delicate points of my elbows poised lightly on the table in the manner my mother had shown me for posing for the press. I would swing my patent leather shoes back and forth like an impatient child riding on a school bus. Then I would pause, suck in my lips, twirl my chosen piece in midair as if undecided, and then firmly plant it in its new threatening place, with a triumphant smile thrown back at my opponent for good measure.

I no longer played in the alley of Waverly Place. I never visited the playground where the pigeons and old men gathered. I went to school, then directly home to learn new chess secrets, cleverly concealed advantages, more escape routes.

But I found it difficult to concentrate at home. My mother had a habit of standing over me while I plotted out my games. I think she thought of herself as my protective ally. Her lips would be sealed tight, and after each move I made, a soft "Hmmmmph" would escape from her nose.

"Ma, I can't practice when you stand there like that," I said one day. She retreated to the kitchen and made loud noises with the pots and pans. When the crashing stopped, I could see out of the corner of my eye that she was standing in the doorway. "Hmmmph!" Only this one came out of her tight throat.

My parents made many concessions to allow me to practice. One time I complained that the bedroom I shared was so noisy that I couldn't think. Thereafter, my brothers slept in a bed in the living room facing the street. I said I couldn't finish my rice; my head didn't work right when my stomach was too full. I left the table with half-finished bowls and nobody complained. But there was one duty I couldn't avoid. I had to accompany my mother on Saturday market days when I had no tournament to play. My mother would proudly walk with me, visiting many shops, buying very little. "This my daughter Wave-ly Jong," she said to whoever looked her way.

One day, after we left a shop I said under my breath, "I wish you wouldn't do that, telling everybody I'm your daughter." My mother stopped walking. Crowds of people with heavy bags pushed past us on the sidewalk, bumping into first one shoulder, then another.

"Aiii-ya. So shame be with mother?" She grasped my hand even tighter as she glared at me.

I looked down. "It's not that, it's just so obvious. It's just so embarrassing."

"Embarrass you be my daughter?" Her voice was cracking with anger.

"That's not what I meant. That's not what I said."

"What you say?"

I knew it was a mistake to say anything more, but I heard my voice speaking. "Why do you have to use me to show off? If you want to show off, then why don't you learn to play chess?"

My mother's eyes turned into dangerous black slits. She had no words for me, just sharp silence.

I felt the wind rushing around my hot ears. I jerked my hand out of my mother's tight grasp and spun around, knocking into an old woman. Her bag of groceries spilled to the ground.

"Aii-ya! Stupid girl!" my mother and the woman cried. Oranges and tin cans careened down the sidewalk. As my mother stooped to help the old woman pick up the escaping food, I took off.

I raced down the street, dashing between people, not looking back as my mother screamed shrilly, "Meimei! Meimei!" I fled down an alley, past dark curtained shops and merchants washing the grime off their windows. I sped into the sunlight, into a large street crowded with tourists examining trinkets and souvenirs. I ducked into another dark alley, down another street, up another alley. I ran until it hurt and I realized I had nowhere to go, that I was not running from anything. The alleys contained no escape routes.

My breath came out like angry smoke. It was cold. I sat down on an upturned plastic pail next to a stack of empty boxes, cupping my chin with my hands, thinking hard. I imagined my mother, first walking briskly down one street or another looking for me, then giving up and returning home to await my arrival. After two hours, I stood up on creaking legs and slowly walked home.

The alley was quiet and I could see the yellow lights shining from our flat like two tigers' eyes in the night. I climbed the sixteen steps to the door, advancing quietly up each so as not to make any warning sounds. I turned the knob; the door was locked. I heard a chair moving, quick steps, the locks turning—click! click! click!—and then the door opened.

"About time you got home," said Vincent. "Boy, are you in trouble."

He slid back to the dinner table. On a platter were the remains of a large fish, its fleshy head still connected to bones swimming upstream in vain escape. Standing there waiting for my punishment, I heard my mother speak in a dry voice.

"We not concerning this girl. This girl not have concerning for us."

Nobody looked at me. Bone chopsticks clinked against the insides of bowls being emptied into hungry mouths.

I walked into my room, closed the door, and lay down on my bed. The room was dark, the ceiling filled with shadows from the dinnertime lights of neighboring flats.

In my head, I saw a chessboard with sixty-four black and white squares. Opposite me was my opponent, two angry black slits. She wore a triumphant smile. "Strongest wind cannot be seen," she said.

Her black men advanced across the plane, slowly marching to each successive level as a single unit. My white pieces screamed as they scurried and fell off the board one by one. As her men drew closer to my edge, I felt myself growing light. I rose up into the air and flew out the window. Higher and higher, above the alley, over the tops of tiled roofs, where I was gathered up by the wind and pushed up toward the night sky until everything below me disappeared and I was alone.

I closed my eyes and pondered my next move.

THINKING ABOUT IT

1

The door opens and Waverly hears, "Boy, are you in trouble." Will Waverly be able to make peace with her mother? What will be her next move?

2

Many writers for young adults choose the short story form for their work. If you were writing for others your age, what forms of writing would your work take? Tell why.

3

What can we learn from playing games? Choose a game you know and tell what it might teach a person about living.

Another Book About Values

Like Waverly, Clara is searching for values in *Cute Is a Four-Letter Word* by Stella Pevsner. She has set her goals for eighth grade: polish her looks, get on the Pom Pon squad, and attract Skip Svoboda, basketball star. Clara finds out that some goals are more important than others.

BY PATRICIA MACLACHLAN

ALL THE NAMES
OF BABY HAG

isten. *Do you hear it? That soft wet sound when the waves come in and slide back again? It is the whisper of the sea hags, soft and sly. An every-so-often whisper as they come up from the sea and disguise themselves—a rest from the tiresome peace under the water, the boring rise and fall, in and out of the tides. You have seen the hags, yes you have, don't shake your head. The leather-faced, chicken-legged women with gold chains yelling, "Stop throwing sand, Dwight. This very minute. I meeean it!" Sea hags. The old man with the bucket belly who sleeps with his face to the sun, mouth open, awakening suddenly with a drool. A sea hag. The silent child who visits your beach blanket and eats up your french fries before you notice. Sea hag.*

Baby Sea Hag was born in the stillness of a slack tide. She was round and the pale-green color of a sea urchin, with delicate diaphanous fins and tidy webbed feet.

"Lovely hag," Mother Hag murmured. "Like the others."

Father Hag nodded, his long whiskers trailing in the sea. Baby Hag reached out to touch one.

"I wonder what she will choose for her name," mused Father Hag.

"She will find the special name, all her own, just for her," said Mother Hag. "All sea hags do, after all. She will, too."

Baby Hag's brothers and sisters, dozens of them, came from the eel grasses and tidal pools and marshes to see her. They filled the water with breath bubbles that brushed her nose and made her sneeze. Like Baby Hag they were all perfect and pale-green-round, with fins and webbed feet. But Baby Hag was different. She smiled from the moment she was born, for one thing. And she laughed out loud before a full day had passed, unusual for hags. They are generally purposeful and serious-minded creatures. Not frivolous. Certainly not cheerful on a daily basis.

"All the time she's happy!" exclaimed Baby Hag's sister, Snow White Hag. She had found her name when she was disguised as a child, sitting on the edge of a blanket with other children. She had listened to tales read from a book, eating soft white-bread sandwiches with the crusts cut off, seven sweet pickles, and the last lemon sour ball. She had loved that story of human creatures and the sound of the two words that would become her name. The two words that meant the same. Snow. White.

"I thought she was your sister," one boy complained to the other after she'd gone.

"*Mine!* Isn't she *yours?* She ate all the pickles!"

Rex, the oldest of the hag children, swam in circles while Baby Hag trailed behind. "Special she may be," he said, "but she will have to find her own name the way we all did. Up on the land." Rex had spent one lively morning with a large loping black Labrador whose tag read: *Rex is ours. Send him home. We love him.* Rex had loved the dog's sweet, sloppy nature. He had taken him home. And at the end of the day slipped back to the sea with his name.

"Land is far better than the sea for names," said Beach Pea shyly. "Nothing is nameless on land. Children, buildings—humans often name their houses, do you believe it?—and their boats!" Often, when the blooms came, Beach Pea went up to the shore, disguised as a toad or a child, a sand flea or a grandmother, to peer at the pink-lavender bloom of the beach pea. "Even cars they name," she added. "Chevrolet. Chev-ro-lay. Lovely, don't you think, Chevrolet?"

Baby Hag smiled.

"She likes it!" cried Beach Pea.

"She does," said Mother Hag, matter-of-factly. "She likes Mirabelle, Clothilde, and Veronica, too. And Baby Bernice."

"All of them?" asked Father Hag, amazed.

"All of them."

"What about Olivia?" suggested Beach Pea. "I met an Olivia once when I was a hungry human standing in line for a hamburger."

"Ah, hamburger," said Father Hag softly, remembering his time ashore. He had taken the form of a parking attendant. "I once ate seven. Odd things, hamburgers."

"Mirabelle?"

"Clothilde?"

"Veronica?"

Baby Hag smiled at the names.

"Olivia?"

"Hamburger?" Father Hag's suggestion.

Baby Hag smiled.

"Pippit? A lively and restless name."

"Grandma Meeker? She fished at night by lantern light."

"Elizabeth Margaret Bernadette Mary O'Shaughnessy? She was very bad mannered. She licked all the sandwiches and had to sit the afternoon on a towel."

Still Baby Hag smiled.

"She likes all the names," said Mother Hag. "Strange. Or worse, unnatural."

Father Hag touched Baby Hag very lightly with a fin. "She likes one name as well as another, it seems," he said.

And she did. So the other young hags, the dozens of brothers and sisters, all of them generally purposeful and serious-minded hags, went back to their generally pur-poseful and serious-minded lives. And Baby Hag did not have a name. She didn't have one name, that is. She answered to any and all names. Names that the sea hags had heard on land, crouched in the dune grass, listening; lying on beach blankets, pretending sleep; standing in food lines with handfuls of human food with the strange names. *Onion ring. Chili dog. Submarine. Shake.*

Each day Mother Hag tried out new names.

"Dilly?"

"What?"

"Trixie?"

"Here I am."

"Cousin Coot!"

"Coming!"

"This is impossible," said Mother Hag, crossly. "There is no living hag without a name. Never in hag history has there been a nameless hag!"

"There is now," said Father Hag very softly.

"It cannot go on," said Mother Hag. "It will not go on!"

But it did. The tides rose and fell with magical monotony, and Baby Hag rose and fell, slept and wakened with them. She was left with the lovely light of the sea at dawn, and the dark of it at night. With no names. With *all* names. *Melissa, Sandcastle, Nanny, Umbrella, Myna, Sunrise* . . .

One season led to another—autumn to winter with dark seas and wind, and the rumble of rocks beneath the waves. *Gloria, Alice-Iris, Zoë, Aunt Zell, Sunset* . . .

Not many creatures roamed the land when it was winter; only someone walking now and then, a dog or two or three, and the raccoons at nighttime. Once there was a kite flyer, high in the dunes, and Snow White Hag went up to ask her name. One moment there was nothing but sea and rocks and a great wave. The next moment there was a small, pale child bundled up against the cold.

"My name? Doodoo Schwartz the Third," the kite flyer told Snow White Hag without looking. "*Doo* Schwartz the Third for short." Above, the kite whirled and dipped and fluttered in the winter wind. When she looked again to see who'd asked for her name there was no child. *No child at all*.

"Doodoo Schwartz is nice," Baby Hag told Snow White Hag. "Third is nice, too." She swam in circles, upside down, so that the late sunlight warmed her pale underbelly. "All nice."

"She *is* different, Baby Hag is," said one hag to another. "Liking all those names, not one her own . . . and all that cheer!"

"She will change," said Mother Hag, worried.

"Maybe," said Father Hag. He did not look worried, but he was. Sea hags, purposeful and serious-minded, always worried.

Winter turned to spring and spring to summer, with the great warm sea surrounding Baby Hag. Father Hag

watched Baby Hag closely. He swam with the currents, Baby Hag following always, and went about his life thinking about names. He thought very hard, as if one name—just one name of all the names—might float like a bubble into Baby Hag's mind. Or heart. *Lucy, Chloe, Afton, Wild Annie . . .*

Rex went up to land as a beagle, his face to the ground, sniffing out names like a dog nosing for food. Beach Pea went, too, though no one knew what form she took. She visited a garden.

"How about Runner Bean?" she suggested. "Or Rosa Ragosa—wild blooms by the sea. Or . . ." She swam close to whisper to Baby Hag, "Eggplant! Luminous during the full moon, and firm bodied."

Baby Hag liked Luminous.

Rex returned breathless after two days. He had raced the beaches and sea roads with two dogs, in and out of the wild honeysuckle, up and down the dunes, back and forth through steaming compost heaps; sending up flocks of quail, chasing cats whose hair stood in ridges along their backs. At dusk chewing on old bones.

Rex sighed and treaded water wearily.

"A waste of time," he announced. "One was a tiresome terrier whose name you wouldn't want. The small one was too low to the ground and had a flat forehead. Lady? Scruffy?"

Baby Hag shook her head.

Snow White Hag sighed.

"You must have a name," she said sadly. "A name that means you."

"*My* name means me," said Beach Pea thoughtfully. "Sometimes, just before sleep, I think about the color of the wild blooms against the sand. And the soft feel of them."

"I think about Rex on land even in daylight," said Rex. "I see him in the eye of my mind stalking cars, rolling by the water in the carcass of a dead cod; twitching his legs in his dreams."

"I know," said Baby Hag, nodding her head up and down. "Lots of names mean me. All names. If I have one name, you know, I cannot have another. If I am Veronica I can't be Eggplant. And if I come when you call Clothilde I can't when you call Pippit."

"No," said Mother Hag fiercely. "I am weary of this. It is not the way of hags. One hag, one name. And that is that!"

There was a silence that grew slowly like the full-moon tide filling a marsh. Even Rex, sometimes as easygoing as a mutt, was silent and serious.

"The first fair day," said Mother Hag firmly, "you will go up to land and find a name. There will be a long, warm shore full of names."

"Many names," agreed Baby Hag cheerfully. "All names."

At this Mother Hag lost all reason.

"Not all names!" she cried. With every word a burst of bubbles came forth. "The first name you hear. *That* will be your name. Then you will return to the sea and we'll all live in peace." She looked at Baby Hag and her face softened a bit. "And you will have one name. One name that means you."

The sun had faded long ago. Night moved overhead, and slowly, without a word, the other hags swam off. They would return with the sun.

One name. Only one name Mother Hag wanted for Baby Hag; Baby Hag wished for all names. Impossible. One name. All names. It became a song that sang in Father Hag's head, over and over. He closed his eyes and rocked gently in the sea. One name. All names. *The first name she heard*. Impossible. *Or was it?* Suddenly Father Hag opened his eyes in the darkness. He smiled. It was strange to him, the smiling, though it felt familiar like a sudden smell from the past, a glimpse of something nearly, but not quite, forgotten. The night rains came, and the soft dropping on the water finally lulled him to sleep. He smiled all through his dreams.

Morning bloomed bright. There were dogs by the sea, and children with their pants rolled, chasing waves.

"Now," Mother Hag said to Baby Hag. "Quickly before the other hag children come. Go up to land for your name."

Father Hag smiled at Baby Hag and nodded his head.

Baby Hag peered at him. There was something. Something about his eyes that made her smile, too.

"Will you come with me?" she asked.

Father Hag shook his head.

"You will be fine. Remember, the first name you hear."

Baby Hag nodded, and with a quick flash of fin she swam to the surface of the sea. Into the first rise of wave she went, over and onto the next, and to the next. Six waves she rode, and then, with a great rush of foam and rolling wave and the barest whisper of sound, she tumbled onto wet sand—a small child blinking in the sunlight. It was strange on land, warm and bright. There was no safe darkness of the sea, no brothers and sisters. For the first time she felt earth beneath her feet.

Nearby sat a child, building a sand castle, humming to herself; another was throwing sand; a mother asleep, a father calling. Baby Hag turned around with a start, and there stood a child staring at her. The child's hair was short, and it was hard to tell if it was a boy child or girl. The child moved closer, closer, until it stood a breath away, arms folded, a small string of jingle shells strung in a bracelet on one wrist. Baby Hag tried to look away. But there was something about the child's eyes. Suddenly the child reached out and touched Baby Hag lightly, very lightly, and the string of jingle shells made a

soft sweet noise. *Something about the eyes*. Baby Hag stared at the child. She took a deep breath.
And she spoke.

"What is your name?"

She had never heard her own voice out of the sea. It seemed to fly away like spindrift.

The child smiled.

"Guess," said the child.

Guess.

In that moment the wind died and there was a great stillness between one wave and another. Baby Hag smiled at the child. And with a small sound, with the next wave, Baby Hag was gone.

"Was that a child?" called a woman nearby, looking alarmed. "Where did that child go?"

A man shook his head.

"Who was she? What was her name?"

They both turned to ask the other child. But the other child was gone, too. *There was no child at all.*

Her name? Baby Hag heard the question and swam wave past wave past wave, slipping down again through the cool waters of her home. Down where her family waited for her.

"What is it?" called Rex, excited.

"Your name?" asked Mother Hag.

Baby Hag smiled at them.

"Guess," she said.

"Clothilde?"

"Martine?"

"No," said Baby Hag, shaking her head. "Guess."

"Lila?"

"Lizzie?"

A slight brush of fins touched Baby Hag then, and her father was there beside her.

"She has told you her name," he said. "It is not Clothilde or Francine, Lila or Lizzie. Her name," he said slowly, "is Guess."

There was a silence. Rex was the first to speak.

"Guess," he said. He laughed. "Guess."

"One name," said Mother Hag softly.

"One name for those who know her," said Father Hag. "But from those who ask her, she will always hear all the names she loves."

Baby Hag . . . Guess . . . turned to look at Father Hag, and she smiled suddenly at what she saw. Around one fin, so delicate that it moved in the currents of the water, hung a string of white jingle shells.

There it is, that whisper again! Hush, and you may hear another. It may be a child who appears suddenly, silently behind you, or a dog who grins. If the dog follows you, quickly tell him your name and he will trot away. If the child asks your name, do not say Guess. There is already a Guess who smiles and dreams beneath the sea. She lives with the lovely light of the sea at dawn, and the dark of it at night. With one name. With all names. And one thing more. Around her neck she wears a slim thread necklace of jingle shells.

How Do Story Ideas Begin?

by Patricia MacLachlan

Patricia MacLachlan

I don't often write fantasy, though I've always known that from fantasy and fairy tales spring great truths. Sometimes fantasy allows us to explore subjects that are important to us, in a humorous and disguised way. We can become a toad or a talking dog or, in this case, a creature from the sea.

The story "All the Names of Baby Hag" came from three separate events. I have a house by the sea on Cape Cod and have spent hours at the shore, the writer and spy in me wondering about the lives of people there: the grumpy child arguing with a grumpy mother, the family laughing together on the next beach blanket, the happy dog that races into the waves to retrieve a stick. Once, at a neighborhood clambake, a woman came out of the water in an expensive bathing suit, with many gold chains around her wrinkled neck. A friend of my son's commented, "A sea hag," and in my head the story began.

Names have always fascinated me, too: family names, the names of dogs and cats and horses, the names of towns and states, as well as the titles of books. As a child, I was always disappointed in my name and wished to be Lucy, or something romantic like Anemone or Clothilde.

The most personal story source for "All the Names of Baby Hag," however, was my favorite uncle who, when he was a child, named his dog Guess. "What's your dog's name?" people would ask him. "Guess," he would say, and they would call up hundreds of names as he shook his head and calmly repeated, "No, Guess."

THINKING
ABOUT IT

1

What's in a name? What is really in a name? As you read "All the Names of Baby Hag," what *reflections* did you have about names?

2

What do sea hags (in the water) look like? How do they sound when they talk? How do you use the story's clues to see and hear them in your mind? Explain.

3

Father Hag, Mother Hag, Snow White, Rex, Sweet Pea, and Guess all go on land one day. Plan a "shore day" for them. Where will they go? What will they do? What will they eat? Tell why you make the plans that you do.

THE NAMING OF CATS
by T. S. Eliot

The Naming of Cats is a difficult matter,
    It isn't just one of your holiday games;
You may think at first I'm as mad as a hatter
When I tell you, a cat must have THREE DIFFERENT
    NAMES.
First of all, there's the name that the family use daily,
    Such as Peter, Augustus, Alonzo or James,
Such as Victor or Jonathan, George or Bill Bailey—
    All of them sensible everyday names.
There are fancier names if you think they sound sweeter,
    Some for the gentlemen, some for the dames:
Such as Plato, Admetus, Electra, Demeter—
    But all of them sensible everyday names.
But I tell you, a cat needs a name that's particular,
    A name that's peculiar, and more dignified,
Else how can he keep up his tail perpendicular,
    Or spread out his whiskers, or cherish his pride?
Of names of this kind, I can give you a quorum,
    Such as Munkustrap, Quaxo, or Coricopat,
Such as Bombalurina, or else Jellylorum—

Names that never belong to more than one cat.
But above and beyond there's still one name left over,
  And that is the name that you never will guess;
The name that no human research can discover—
  But THE CAT HIMSELF KNOWS, and will never confess.
When you notice a cat in profound meditation,
  The reason, I tell you, is always the same:
His mind is engaged in a rapt contemplation
  Of the thought, of the thought, of the thought
    of his name:
  His ineffable effable
  Effanineffable
Deep and inscrutable singular Name.

BY ALEX HALEY

FAR FROM THE BAOBAB TREE

FROM ROOTS

A s a boy growing up in Henning, Tennessee, Alex Haley listened to his grandmother's family stories about an ancestor many generations back whom she referred to as "the African." He was named 'Kin-tay' and had lived near the 'Kamby Bolongo.' He had been out in the forest one day chopping wood to make himself a drum when he was captured, beaten, bound in chains, and sent aboard a slave ship to America.

As an adult and a writer, Haley began to trace the African names and words which had been passed down in his grandmother's stories. Ten years of research, travel, and writing later, he had authenticated two centuries of his family history and written a best seller (Roots) which was later made into a TV miniseries. One of the most exciting points of Haley's search was his location of the Kinte clan of which he was a member in The Gambia, Africa.

I had a long talk with George Sims, with whom I'd grown up in Henning, and who is a master researcher. After a few days, George brought me a list of about a dozen people academically renowned for their knowledge of African linguistics. One whose background intrigued me quickly was a Belgian, Dr. Jan Vansina. After study at the University of London's School of African and Oriental Studies, he had done his early work living in African villages and written a book called *La Tradition Orale*. I telephoned Dr. Vansina where he now taught at the University of Wisconsin, and he gave me an appointment to see him. It was a Wednesday morning that I flew to Madison, Wisconsin, motivated by my intense curiosity about some strange phonetic sounds . . . and with no dream in this world of what was about to start happening . . .

That evening in the Vansinas' living room, I told him every syllable I could remember of the family narrative heard since little boyhood—recently buttressed by Cousin Georgia in Kansas City. Dr. Vansina, after listening intently throughout, then began asking me questions. Being an oral historian, he was particularly interested in the physical transmission of the narrative down across generations.

We talked so late that he invited me to spend the night, and the next morning Dr. Vansina, with a very serious expression on his face, said, "I wanted to sleep on it. The ramifications of phonetic sounds preserved down across your family's generations can be immense." He said that he had been on the phone with a colleague Africanist, Dr. Philip Curtin; they both felt certain that the sounds I'd conveyed to him were from the "Mandinka" tongue. I'd never heard that word; he told me that it was the language spoken by the Mandingo people. Then he guess translated certain of the sounds. One of them probably meant cow or cattle; another probably meant the baobab tree, generic in West Africa. The word *ko,* he said, could refer to the *kora,* one of the Mandingo people's oldest stringed instruments, made of a halved large dried gourd covered with goatskin, with a long neck, and twenty-one strings with a bridge. An enslaved Mandingo might relate the *kora* visually to some among the types of stringed instruments that U.S. slaves had.

The most involved sound I had heard and brought was Kamby Bolongo, my ancestor's sound to his daughter Kizzy as he had pointed to the Matta-poni River in Spotsylvania County, Virginia. Dr. Vansina said that without question, *bolongo* meant, in the Mandinka tongue, a moving water, as a river; preceded by "Kamby," it could indicate the Gambia River.

I'd never heard of it.

An incident happened that would build my feel-ing—especially as more uncanny things occurred—that, yes, they were up there watchin' . . .

I was asked to speak at a seminar held at Utica College, Utica, New York. Walking down a hallway with the professor who had invited me, I said I'd just flown in from Washington and why I'd been there. "The Gambia? If I'm not mistaken, someone men-tioned recently that an outstanding student from that country is over at Hamilton."

The old, distinguished Hamilton College was maybe a half hour's drive away, in Clinton, New York. Before I could finish asking, a Professor Charles Todd said, "You're talking about Ebou Manga." Consulting a course roster, he told me where I could find him in an agricultural economics class. Ebou Manga was small of build, with careful eyes, a reserved manner, and black as soot. He tentatively confirmed my sounds, clearly startled to have heard me uttering them. Was Mandinka his home tongue? "No, although I am familiar with it." He was a Wolof, he said. In his dormitory room, I told him about my quest. We left for The Gambia at the end of the following week.

Arriving in Dakar, Senegal, the next morning, we caught a light plane to small Yundum Airport in The Gambia. In a passenger van, we rode into the capital city of Banjul (then Bathurst). Ebou and his father, Alhaji Manga—Gambians are mostly Moslem—assembled a small group of men knowledgeable in their small country's history, who met with me in the lounge of the Atlantic Hotel. As I had told Dr. Vansina in Wisconsin, I told these men the family narrative that had come down across the generations. I told them in a reverse progression, backward from Grandma through Tom, Chicken George, then Kizzy saying how her African father insisted to other slaves that his name was "Kin-tay," and repetitively told her phonetic sounds identifying various things, along with stories such as that he had been attacked and seized while not far from his village, chopping wood.

When I had finished, they said almost with wry amusement, "Well, of course 'Kamby Bolongo' would mean Gambia River; anyone would know that." I told them hotly that no, a great many people *wouldn't* know it! Then they showed a much greater interest that my 1760s ancestor had insisted his name was "Kin-tay." "Our country's oldest villages tend to be named for the families that settled those villages centuries ago," they said. Sending for a map, pointing, they said, "Look, here is the village of Kinte-Kundah. And not too far from it, the village of Kinte-Kundah Janneh-Ya."

Then they told me something of which I'd never have dreamed: of very old men, called *griots*,[1] still to be found in the older back-country villages, men who were in effect living, walking archives of oral history. A senior *griot* would be a man usually in his late sixties or early seventies; below him would be progressively younger *griots*—and apprenticing boys, so a boy would be exposed to those *griots'* particular line of narrative for forty or fifty years before he could qualify as a senior *griot,* who told on special occasions the centuries-old histories of villages, of clans, of families, of great heroes. Throughout the whole of black Africa such oral chronicles had been handed down since the time of the ancient forefathers, I was informed, and there were certain legendary *griots* who could narrate facets of African history literally for as long as three days without ever repeating themselves.

Seeing how astounded I was, these Gambian men reminded me that every living person ancestrally goes

---

[1]*griots* (grē ōz′)

back to some time and some place where no writing existed; and then human memories and mouths and ears were the only ways those human beings could store and relay information. They said that we who live in the Western culture are so conditioned to the "crutch of print" that few among us comprehend what a trained memory is capable of.

Since my forefather had said his name was "Kintay"—properly spelled "Kinte," they said—and since the Kinte clan was old and well known in The Gambia, they promised to do what they could to find a *griot* who might be able to assist my search.

Back in the United States, I began devouring books on African history. It grew quickly into some kind of obsession to correct my ignorance concerning the earth's second-largest continent. It embarrasses me to this day that up to then my images about Africa had been largely derived or inferred from Tarzan movies and my very little authentic knowledge had come from only occasional leafings through the *National Geographic*. All of a sudden now, after reading all day, I'd sit on the edge of my bed at night studying a map of Africa, memorizing the different countries' relative positions and the principal waters where slave ships had operated.

After some weeks, a registered letter came from The Gambia; it suggested that when possible, I should come back. But by now I was stony broke— especially because I'd been investing very little of my time in writing.

Once at a *Reader's Digest* lawn party, cofounder Mrs. Dewit Wallace had told me how much she liked an "Unforgettable Character" I had written—about a tough old seadog cook who had once been my boss in the U. S. Coast Guard—and before leaving, Mrs. Wallace volunteered that I should let her know if I

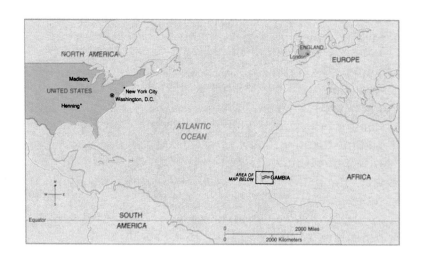

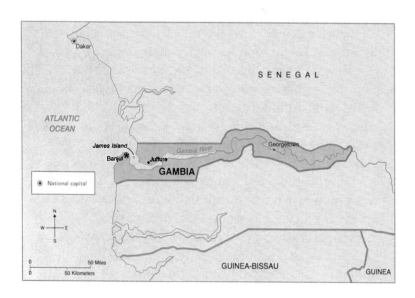

In 1965, The Gambia became an independent country with an elected president. The Mandingo people are the largest of the five main ethnic groups there. They are tall, music-loving people who are mostly traders and peanut farmers.

ever needed some help. Now I wrote to Mrs. Wallace a rather embarrassed letter, briefly telling her the compulsive quest I'd gotten myself into. She asked some editors to meet with me and see what they felt, and invited to lunch with them, I talked about non-stop for nearly three hours. Shortly afterward, a letter told me that the *Reader's Digest* would provide me with a three-hundred-dollar monthly check for one year, and plus that—my really vital need—"reasonable necessary travel expenses."

I again visited Cousin Georgia in Kansas City— something had urged me to do so, and I found her quite ill. But she was thrilled to hear both what I had learned and what I hoped to learn. She wished me Godspeed, and I flew then to Africa.

The same men with whom I had previously talked told me now in a rather matter-of-fact manner that they had caused word to be put out in the back country, and that a *griot* very knowledgeable of the Kinte clan had indeed been found—his name, they said, was "Kebba Kanji Fofana." I was ready to have a fit. "Where *is* he?" They looked at me oddly: "He's in his village."

I discovered that if I intended to see this *griot,* I was going to have to do something I'd never have dreamed I'd ever be doing—organizing what seemed, at least to me then, a kind of minisafari! It took me three days of negotiating through unaccustomed endless African palaver finally to hire a launch to get upriver; to rent a lorry and a Land-Rover to take supplies by a roundabout land route; to hire finally a total of fourteen people, including three interpreters and four musicians, who had told me that the old *griots* in the back country wouldn't talk without music in the background.

In the launch *Baddibu,* vibrating up the wide, swift "Kamby Bolongo," I felt queasily, uncomfortably alien. Did they all have me appraised as merely another pith helmet? Finally ahead was James Island, for two centuries the site of a fort over which England and France waged war back and forth for the ideal vantage point to trade in slaves. Asking if we might land there awhile, I trudged amid the crumbling ruins yet guarded by ghostly cannon. Picturing in my mind the kinds of atrocities that would have happened there, I felt as if I would like to go flailing an ax back through that facet of black Africa's history. Without luck I tried to find for myself some symbol remnant of an ancient chain, but I took a chunk of mortar and a brick. In the next minutes before we returned to the *Baddibu,* I just gazed up and down that river that my ancestor had named for his daughter far across the Atlantic Ocean in Spotsylvania County, Virginia. Then we went on, and upon arriving at a little village called Albreda, we put ashore, our destination now on foot the yet smaller village of Juffure, where the men had been told that this *griot* lived.

There is an expression called "the peak experience"—that which emotionally, nothing in your life ever transcends. I've had mine, that first day in the back country of black West Africa.

When we got within sight of Juffure, the children who were playing outside gave the alert, and the people came flocking from their huts. It's a village of only about seventy people. Like most back-country villages, it was still very much as it was two hundred years ago, with its circular mud houses and their conical thatched roofs. Among the people as they gathered was a small man wearing an off-white robe, a pillbox hat over an aquiline-featured black face, and about him was an aura of "somebodiness" until I knew he was the man we had come to see and hear.

As the three interpreters left our party to converge upon him, the seventy-odd other villagers gathered closely around me, in a kind of horseshoe pattern, three or four deep all around; had I stuck out my arms, my fingers would have touched the nearest ones on either side. They were all staring at me. The eyes just raked me. Their foreheads were furrowed with their very intensity of staring. A kind of visceral surging or a churning sensation started up deep inside me; bewildered, I was wondering what on earth was this . . . then in a little while it was rather as if some full-gale force of realization rolled in on me: Many times in my life I had been among crowds of people, but never where *every one was jet black!*

Rocked emotionally, my eyes dropped downward as we tend to do when we're uncertain, insecure, and my glance fell upon my own hands' brown complexion. This time more quickly than before, and even harder, another gale-force emotion hit me: I felt myself some variety of a hybrid . . . I felt somehow impure among the pure; it was a terribly shaming feeling. About then, abruptly the old man left the interpreters. The people immediately also left me now to go crowding about him.

One of my interpreters came up quickly and whispered in my ears, "They stare at you so much because they have never here seen a black American." When I grasped the significance, I believe that hit me harder than what had already happened. They hadn't been looking at me as an individual, but I represented in their eyes a symbol of the twenty-five millions of us black people whom they had never seen, who lived beyond an ocean.

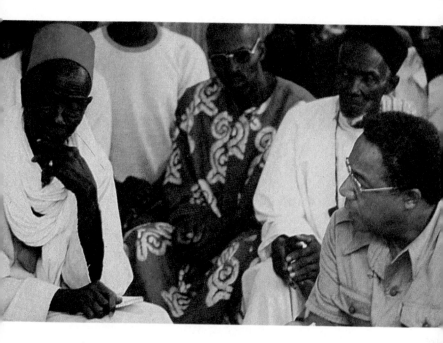

The people were clustered thickly about the old man, all of them intermittently flicking glances toward me as they talked animatedly in their Mandinka tongue. After a while, the old man turned, walked briskly through the people, past my three interpreters, and right up to me. His eyes piercing into mine, seeming to feel I should understand his Mandinka, he expressed what they had all decided they *felt* concerning those unseen millions of us who lived in those places that had been slave ships' destinations—and the translation came: "We have been told by the forefathers that there are many of us from this place who are in exile in that place called America—and in other places."

The old man sat down, facing me, as the people hurriedly gathered behind him. Then he began to recite for me the ancestral history of the Kinte clan, as it had been passed along orally down across centuries from the forefathers' time. It was not merely conversational, but more as if a scroll were being read; for the still, silent villagers, it was clearly a formal occasion. The *griot* would speak, bending forward from the waist, his body rigid, his neck cords standing out, his words seeming almost physical objects. After a sentence or two, seeming to go limp, he would lean back, listening to an interpreter's translation. Spilling from the *griot's* head came an incredibly complex Kinte clan lineage that reached back across many generations: who married whom; who had what children; what children then married whom; then their offspring. It was all just unbelievable. I was struck not only by the profusion of details, but also by the narrative's biblical style, something like: "—and so-and-so took as a wife so-and-so, and begat . . . and begat . . . and begat . . ." He would next name each begat's eventual spouse, or spouses, and their averagely numerous offspring, and so on. To date things the *griot* linked them to events, such as "—in the year of the big water"—a flood—"he slew a water buffalo." To determine the calendar date, you'd have to find out when that particular flood occurred.

Simplifying to its essence the encyclopedic saga that I was told, the *griot* said that the Kinte clan had begun in the country called Old Mali. Then the Kinte men traditionally were blacksmiths, "who had conquered fire," and the women mostly were potters and weavers. In time, one branch of the clan moved into the country called Mauretania; and it was from Mauretania that one son of this clan, whose name was Kairaba Kunta Kinte—a *marabout,* or holy man of the Moslem faith—journeyed down into the country called The Gambia. He went first to a village called Pakali N'Ding, stayed there for a while, then went to a village called Jiffarong, and then to the village of Juffure.

In Juffure, Kairaba Kunta Kinte took his first wife, a Mandinka maiden whose name was Sireng. And by her he begot two sons, whose names were Janneh and Saloum. Then he took a second wife; her name was Yaisa. And by Yaisa, he begot a son named Omoro.

Those three sons grew up in Juffure until they became of age. Then the elder two, Janneh and Saloum, went away and founded a new village called Kinte-Kundah Janneh-Ya. The youngest son, Omoro, stayed on in Juffure village until he had thirty rains—years—of age, then he took as his wife a Mandinka maiden named Binta Kebba. And by Binta Kebba, roughly between the years 1750 and 1760, Omoro Kinte begat four sons, whose names were, in the order of their birth, Kunta, Lamin, Suwadu, and Madi.

The old *griot* had talked for nearly two hours up to then, and perhaps fifty times the narrative had included some detail about someone whom he had named. Now after he had just named those four sons, again he appended a detail, and the interpreter translated—

"About the time the King's soldiers came"—another of the *griot's* time-fixing references—"the eldest of these four sons, Kunta, went away from his village to chop wood . . . and he was never seen again. . . ." And the *griot* went on with his narrative.

I sat as if I were carved of stone. My blood seemed to have congealed. This man whose lifetime had been in this back-country African village had no way in the world to know that he had just echoed what I had heard all through my boyhood years on my grandma's front porch in Henning, Tennessee . . . of an African who always had insisted that his name was "Kin-tay"; who had called a guitar a "*ko*," and a river within the state of Virginia,

"Kamby Bolongo"; and who had been kidnapped into slavery while not far from his village, chopping wood, to make himself a drum.

I managed to fumble from my dufflebag my basic notebook, whose first pages containing grandma's story I showed to an interpreter. After briefly reading, clearly astounded, he spoke rapidly while showing it to the old *griot,* who became agitated; he got up, exclaiming to the people, gesturing at my notebook in the interpreter's hands, and *they* all got agitated.

I don't remember hearing anyone giving an order, I only recall becoming aware that those seventy-odd people had formed a wide human ring around me, moving counterclockwise, chanting softly, loudly, softly; their bodies close together, they were lifting their knees high, stamping up reddish puffs of the dust. . . .

The woman who broke from the moving circle was one of about a dozen whose infant children were within cloth slings across their backs. Her jet-black face deeply contorting, the woman came charging toward me, her bare feet slapping the earth, and snatching her baby free, she thrust it at me almost roughly, the gesture saying "Take it!" . . . and I did, clasping the baby to me. Then she snatched away her baby; and another woman was thrusting her baby, then another, and another . . . until I had embraced probably a dozen babies. I wouldn't learn until maybe a year later, from a Harvard University professor, Dr. Jerome Bruner, a scholar of such matters, "You didn't know you were participating in one of the oldest ceremonies of humankind, called 'The laying on of hands'! In their way, they were telling you 'Through this flesh, which is us, we are you, and you are us!'"

THINKING
ABOUT IT

1

When the griot told about Kunta Kinte, Haley said, "I sat as if I were carved of stone. My blood seemed to have congealed." When have you had such an exciting or frightening experience that you were "carved of stone"? Tell your story.

2

Haley was able to trace his family history because he met several key people. Who were those people and how did each help him?

3

You've decided to find out about your family's history. Where do you start? Who can tell you stories or give you information? Where might you look to find the evidence—census records, old letters, birth and death records, old family Bibles? Create a plan for beginning your search.

BY SANDRA CISNEROS

MY NAME

FROM THE HOUSE ON

MANGO STREET

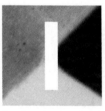 n English my name means hope. In Spanish it means too many letters. It means sadness, it means waiting. It is like the number nine. A muddy color. It is the Mexican records my father plays on Sunday mornings when he is shaving, songs like sobbing.

It was my great-grandmother's name and now it is mine. She was a horse woman too, born like me in the Chinese year of the horse—which is supposed to be bad luck if you're born female—but I think this is a Chinese lie because the Chinese, like the Mexicans, don't like their women strong.

My great-grandmother. I would've liked to have known her, a wild horse of a woman, so wild she wouldn't marry until my great-grandfather threw a sack over her head and carried her off. Just like that, as if she were a fancy chandelier. That's the way he did it.

And the story goes she never forgave him. She looked out the window all her life, the way so many women sit their sadness on an elbow. I wonder if she made the best with what she got or was she sorry because she couldn't be all the things she wanted to be. Esperanza. I have inherited her name, but I don't want to inherit her place by the window.

At school they say my name funny as if the syllables were made out of tin and hurt the roof of your mouth. But in Spanish my name is made out of a softer something like silver, not quite as thick as my sister's name Magdalena which is uglier than mine. Magdalena who at least can come home and become Nenny. But I am always Esperanza.

I would like to baptize myself under a new name, a name more like the real me, the one nobody sees. Esperanza as Lisandra or Maritza or Zeze the X. Yes. Something like Zeze the X will do.

THINKING ABOUT IT

1

As you read this selection, what did you remember about your own name and people's reactions to your name? What did you think about your name? What did you wish? Why?

2

What are Esperanza's major complaints about her name? What would you advise her?

3

Someday, you may have an opportunity to name children of your own. Choose names for two boys and two girls and tell why you've chosen those names.

BY MARY PRICE LEE

FIRST NAMES AROUND THE WORLD

What are some of the different customs in naming a baby around the world? Mothers and fathers worldwide have so many traditions to follow, so many names they can choose from. But to each parent, whatever the tradition, the name given to his or her child makes it the most important baby in the world.

In Japan, children are often numbered instead of named. Ichiko means number one child, or firstborn. Brother number two would be Nichiko. At the age of fifteen, a young boy may take on another name that reflects the social standing of the family or the father's business. A Japanese boy's name, then, may also be a kind of title.

The Nigerian baby is loved and watched over by the entire community. Relatives and neighbors as well as parents welcome the baby into their close-knit society.

The Nigerian (Yoruban) naming ceremony is very special and very beautiful. The family history of the new infant is set forth before the happy crowd gathered for the occasion. And even the spirits of ancestors are welcomed to join the ceremony and bless the child.

The baby is then treated to little tastes of honey, wine, water, salt, and pepper. A bit of each is dropped on the tiny tongue. These represent all the elements needed for a happy life. The honey guarantees happiness; the wine, good wishes; and the water is sustainer of life itself. The salt gives life its flavor, and the pepper its spice. If the baby does not sneeze after a sample of the pepper, he or she is off to a good start!

Francis Selormey, once a director of the Central Organization of Sports in Ghana, remembers the birth of his little sister and her introduction to society. He recalls a very colorful aspect of the time-honored Yoruban naming ceremony: "One of the women in the group rushed forward and picked up the baby saying, 'Whose precious child is this? I have found it. Who will pay me for this child?' My mother then stepped out of her room for the first time and said, 'I will.' She paid a token price of a penny and received her child back." The payment was symbolic—it simply reaffirmed the great value of the child.

The names selected for Nigerian babies have lovely sounds and inspirational meanings. Parents who name their son Oladele (pronounced aw-lah-day-lay) hope that he will bring "honors and wealth" to the home. In naming a baby Folayan, parents know that she will "walk in dignity" all her life.

A child's name is on trial in some African tribes. If the newly named baby frets and cries for several months, it is a sign that the name is not suitable for the child. He is then given another and everyone hopes that he will coo and gurgle to show his approval.

In France it doesn't pay to be original about names. French citizens must choose from a list of selected names for their new baby, or the child will not be recognized by French law. When Jean-Jacques Le Goarnic gave his six children unofficial names, they were denied their citizenship. Adraboaren, Maiwenn, Gwendal, Diwezha, Sklerjenn, and Brann, ages twelve to nineteen, have only recently been recognized by the French government and accepted as citizens. Their father took his case to the World Court and, after a twenty-year struggle, the youngsters are now legal citizens. If Monsieur Le Goarnic had failed in his effort, the six young Le Goarnics would never have been allowed to drive a car in France, marry in their native country, or enlist in the French army.

French law still states that parents must choose names from the official register, but now there are a greater number of acceptable first names. With the approval of foreign names, some nicknames, and different spellings, French parents will soon have almost as much choice as citizens of other countries.

But then there are problems with last names. The Trognons, a French couple, were denied adoption rights unless they were willing to change their last name. Trognon means Core (of a pear or apple) or Stump (of a cabbage) and the judge in the adoption case objected to a name with such meanings. He was afraid that the adopted children would be ridiculed.

American Indian names are melodious and original. When translated, they delight the ear and please the eye. White Shell, Flower-of-the-World, and Looking-Glass Yellow are among the beautiful word names chosen to fit a winsome new baby.

There are many different naming customs among American Indian tribes. These customs enrich the name of an Indian baby with their mystical meanings. For instance, a child may receive an animal name if Father is out hunting during the baby's birth. When Father returns, the child is given the name of the animal killed during the hunt.

Sometimes an Indian child is named after an event in a dream. Other children have two names, one for winter and one for summer. Some names may be loaned out as the child grows up, while others may be given away if their owners are in the market for another. The young Indian who is quite happy with his birth name may suddenly decide to exchange it for a military title. A pretty Indian lass who answers to Rain-in-the-Face may change her name to fit her new occupation—in translation, Dry Goods Woman.

Some American Indians collect names as others would collect charms for a bracelet. It is not unusual for an Indian child to have nine or ten names, each bestowed upon him or her to mark important occasions.

Many American Indians have names of the English-speaking world. A William or a Katherine is not unusual for an Indian babe. But tribes like the Yakima Indians of the State of Washington retain the right to bestow traditional Indian names through the time-honored ceremonies of formal name-giving.

Brazilians feel that first names are more important than last names. In fact, the Brazilian citizen is sometimes listed in telephone books, civic organizations, and other formal lists by his or her Christian name. Parents often give a child a name that begins with *A* so that the youngster will head the list.

This first-name system would come in handy in our country. Because our last names are inherited, we have no choice about where they fall in the alphabet. So anyone whose name is among the *S*'s to *Z*'s is doomed to bring up the rear every time. But in Brazil, because parents can choose a first name, they can guarantee their child a place near the top. The only problem is that there may be three hundred Anas or Antonios in a telephone book or on a newspaper subscription list.

In Hawaii, boys and girls receive names as rich in meaning as those of the American Indians. But with traditional Hawaiian names there is a difference. Names like My Jewel or Brave One may be used for either a boy or a girl. With the new insistence on equality for women, the old-fashioned Hawaiian names are very useful.

We put titles such as Mr., Ms., Mrs., or Miss at the beginning of names. The Vietnamese do it another way. The middle names of these Oriental people often indicate a boy or a girl, so there is no need for introductory titles. Vietnamese last names, incidentally, are often very short. La, Ta, and Do sound like notes in a musical scale. One thing is certain—they are easy to spell. An American kindergartner learning to spell her name would be delighted to have a two-letter surname. If her last name was Higgenbottom or Raffensperger, she would surely like to trade names with a Vietnamese lass whose last name was Si.

There are many other customs around the world. Here are some of them:

In Purim Kukis in the Minipur State of China, a tightly knit band of residents make their own name rules. If any member of one tribe takes the name of a member of a neighboring tribe, he must hand over a pig and a pot of rice. But once he has handed over these gifts, he is allowed to keep his stolen name.

Many Swedes owe their colorful, warlike names to their Norse ancestors. Their names are full of challenge and bravado—hardly typical of today's peaceful Swedes.

In China, the surnames are written first, the first name last. In America, the names would appear as Anderson John and Jones Lenore.

In Korea, last names come first—sometimes with tragic consequences. Not many years ago, two young Koreans studying in New York met, fell in love, and *then* exchanged names. A name is such a personal thing to the Koreans and many other Orientals that it is not shared until the owner feels comfortable about divulging it.

The two young people, upon learning that they both had the name Kim, were forced to give each other up and seek other mates. Because they each had the identical last name, it was obvious that they had a common male ancestor. It is against Korean law to marry someone to whom you are related on the male side.

In this case, Kim Su Ro, born in A.D. 41, was the common male ancestor of these two unlucky lovers. Legend says that Kim Su Ro was conceived from a golden egg. Golden eggs are often thought of as good-luck symbols. But to a hundred thousand present-day Kims unfortunate enough to fall in love with a fellow Kim, the golden egg is no prize.

In some countries, two is a magic number. That is, twins are considered to be supernatural—not quite like other infants. The Nuer, an African tribe, feel that birds and twins are both very unusual. They honor the rare newborn look-alikes by reserving beautiful bird names for them.

There are many interesting naming customs among the Jews. These are customs that know no homeland, because many Jews all over the world follow them. One tradition follows the rule that the aunt or uncle, grandmother or grandfather has prior ownership to a name. This means that a parent had better find a brand-new one for a newborn.

Some Jews "fence" with the Angel of Death when a new baby is very ill. They feel that there really is such a bad angel, and they try to confuse him. If the wicked Messenger is looking for a little boy named David who is deathly ill, the parents might change the boy's name to

Samuel. The Angel of Death will pass by the sick "Samuel," because he is looking for David to take with him.

Despite the many names and naming customs around the world, there are some things that never change. Parents everywhere take time to name their babies because they love them. And they tend to choose names that have always been popular in their own countries.

Actually, there are several names that are popular in many, many countries. Sometimes these names sound like each other—sometimes they don't. Let's look at Barbara and Richard in countries many travel-hours away from each other.

ENGLISH	Barbara	Richard
CZECH	Barbara	Richard
FRENCH	Barbe	Richard
GERMAN	Barbara	Richard
GREEK	Voska	Rihardos
HUNGARIAN	Barbola	Ricard
ITALIAN	Barbara	Riccardo
LATVIAN	Barbar	Risardas
POLISH	Barbara	Ryszard
PORTUGUESE	Barbara	Ricardo
RUMANIAN	Varvara	Dic
RUSSIAN	Varvara	Rostislav
SERBO-CROATIAN	Varvara	Rihard
SPANISH	Bárbara	Ricardo
SWEDISH	Barbro	Rickard
UKRANIAN	Varvaru	Rostyslav

That's a lot of Barbaras and Richards, or Varvaras and Ricardos!

THINKING
ABOUT IT

1

The government or head of your tribe has just told you that your name is not allowed—for whatever reason—and that you must change it. What is your response?

2

In thinking about all the different ways of naming, which two or three do you like best? What would you name yourself using those ways? If you can, tell why you have the name you have now.

3

You have been named head of your tribe. You are now the leader of your real-life family. How do you name people in your "tribe"? What new names will people in your "real" family get?

BY MARI SANDOZ

FAR LOOKER

hen the son of Tall Deer was born, the Sioux warrior gave away many ponies. He gave ponies to all those of his village who were poor, for was not his son, No Eyes, of the Chosen Ones? Many children came every year to the tipis of the great Sioux people, but only a few were set off from the rest because they would never hear the barking of the village dogs, or learn to make words, or see the sun on the buffalo grass. These, it was well known, were the bearers of great gifts for the preservation of their people. And so Tall Deer made all the village glad with him.

Soon this boy of the Chosen Ones learned to know many things beyond common man. He could feel spring on his cheek when the tipis were yet in snow, could smell the smokeless enemy fire that none could see, could hear the far crunch of the ice under the feet of the elk when meat was low in the village. Often in the night he was allowed to roam, for darkness and day were as one to him.

Then one night the fall he was nine, when the ponies were fat and the village full of winter meat, he smelled the burning of the smokeless fire. He was away from his village, up the wind, and his own people had no reason to burn the fire of the sneaker of the night. Swiftly he thought. It must be an enemy war party, out for horses, meat, and scalps. He sniffed the air, slipped off his moccasins and circled out wide, like the bow of a great man. Then his feet felt pony tracks, many times his toes in number, and the broken earth still moist. He followed the trail, losing the fire smell, finding it again. Several times he put his ear to the earth for the sound of pony feet. At last he found them, many ponies feeding, two men on guard, making low words he did not know, and many sleeping men breathing nearby, many men and no women—a war party.

No Eyes knew what this meant—attack at the first small wind of dawn upon his unsuspecting village, robes waved to scatter the pony herd, whooping warriors riding up the canyon to cut off escape, riding down the tipis of his people, with the twanging of the bow string, the swinging of the war club. Swiftly the boy dropped his robe, slipped into his moccasins and began to run. He ran lightly, not swiftly, knowing he must last, avoiding bush and stone and tree, running along the crest of the ridge as the coyote lopes.

An hour later, before the time for the enemy's coming, there was robe-waving among the ponies of the enemy herd, and wild young Sioux riding the surprised sleepers down. By the time the sun was warm on the face, and the cooking fires burning fine before the tipis, the captured ponies were all admired and divided. Then Tall Deer walked slowly through the village in his noblest blanket of blue cloth with a white banding of beads. He was making a song, calling for his friends to feast with him, for now his son who had been No Eyes would be Far Looker, one whose far seeing had indeed saved his village and his people.

PULLING IT ALL TOGETHER

1

What does it mean to be a Chosen One—in this story and in your own life?

2

ESP, Waverly, Guess—Just listen to those names! In their stories, who knew them best and can tell more about them? Summon one supporting character from each of the three stories; have that character explain why the names ESP, Waverly, and Guess deserve to be in the best of books.

3

What does the following poem say about the importance of one's name? Who in this book would agree? What would these characters offer as advice to Two Swans?

NAME GIVEAWAY
by Phillip William George

That teacher gave me a new name . . . again.
She never even had a feast, or, giveaway!

Still I do not know what "George" means.
and now she calls me: "Phillip."

TWO SWANS ASCENDING FROM STILL
WATERS must be too hard for her to remember.

BOOKS TO ENJOY

Jacob Have I Loved
by Katherine Paterson
Crowell, 1980
Sara Louise, nicknamed Wheeze by her beautiful, gifted twin sister, grows up knowing that she is the plain, unloved, unappreciated sister. On their tiny Chesapeake Bay island, Wheeze's dreams are all crushed while Caroline gets the breaks and the education and the love. Can Sara Louise ever find happiness and a place for herself?

It's Like This, Cat
by Emily Neville
Harper, 1963
Dave has two best friends: one is Nick who is much more interested in girls than Dave is; the other is Cat, a gift from Crazy Old Kate who is known for befriending cats and acting unfriendly to people. Dave knows that he'll never get along with his grouchy, critical father and he'll never be able to stand those silly, giggly girls. But growing up in New York City brings many adventures and many changes.

Shark Beneath the Reef
by Jean Craighead George
Harper, 1989
Tomás is torn between loyalty to his family, which is struggling in the fishing business, and his thirst for an education. Can he make the right decision?

Lost in the Barrens
by Farley Mowat
Little, Brown, 1956
A Canadian and a Cree Indian set off on a great adventure to explore the Arctic. But other Indians and the climate, both hostile, turn the adventure into a struggle for survival that gives both teens a lifetime of experiences.

The War at Home
by Connie Jordan Green
Macmillan, 1989
Mattie finds growing up during World War II filled with problems. When her father accepts a job in Tennessee, the whole family is uprooted from their Kentucky home. Then Virgil, her chauvinistic cousin, comes to stay. Dealing with the death of Virgil's mother and the bombings of Hiroshima and Nagasaki teach both Mattie and Virgil about life . . . and death.

A Book About Names
by Milton Meltzer
Harper, 1984
You probably know that "Mark Twain" was Samuel Clemens's *nom de plume* (pen name). And that "Southpaw" can be a nickname for someone who is left-handed. Where do these names come from? How do people of different cultures choose names? What does *your* name mean? This book will answer such questions and more.

LITERARY TERMS

CHARACTERIZATION **Characterization** is the author's way of showing a character's traits, feelings, and goals. An author can describe a character's appearance, report the character's speech and behavior, describe the reactions of other characters to the person, or reveal the character's thoughts and feelings. In "All the Names of Baby Hag," the author describes Baby Hag's happy disposition and shows her family's reactions to her indecision about a name.

FLASHBACK A **flashback** is an interruption in a story to show an event that happened earlier. A **flashback** may be used to show how a past event influences a character's actions or feelings in the present. The **flashback** in "The Fuller Brush Man" takes Donald back to the good things he remembers about his mother when he was younger. This helps him realize how much she means to him and gives him courage to face her illness.

PLOT The **plot** of a story is the series of related events that show the characters in action. The author arranges these events in some kind of order, or sequence, often forming a chain of causes and effects that lead to an outcome. Most **plots** are based on a conflict that gets resolved by the end of the story. "What Do I Do Now?" is an unusual story because the events of the plot are related through a series of letters. The letters show events in chronological order and resolve Extremely Shy Person's conflict in getting to know Alvin better.

SETTING **Setting** is the time and place in which the events of a story occur. The **setting** may be specific and detailed and introduced at the very beginning of the story, or it may be merely suggested through the use of details scattered throughout the story. If the **setting** is vital to the story, it is called an **integral setting.** In "Rules of the Game" the **setting** of San Francisco's Chinatown is important to show Waverly's Chinese heritage and her mother's cultural beliefs. In other stories, the setting may be relatively unimportant.

SHORT STORY A **short story** is a self-contained, short piece of fiction that commonly focuses on one character or on only a few characters. It describes a single event or a series of events that are closely related. "The Fuller Brush Man" focuses on Donald and his relationship with his sick mother. "Rules of the Game" introduces us to Waverly Jong and her mother. These **short stories** contain important story elements: plot, setting, characterization, and theme.

THEME The main idea or central meaning of a piece of writing is its **theme.** The **theme** is the idea that holds a story together. The **theme** in "What Do I Do Now?" is that people can depend on their own resources to solve problems.

GLOSSARY

Vocabulary from your selections

ad ver sar y (ad′vər ser′ē), *n., pl.* **-sar ies.**
1 person or group opposing or resisting another
or others; antagonist; enemy. **2** person or group
on the other side in a contest; opponent.

am or ous (am′ər əs), *adj.* **1** inclined to love; fond
of making love: *an amorous disposition.* **2** in
love; enamored. **3** showing love; loving: *an amorous letter.* **4** having to do with love or court-
ship.

an ces tor (an′ses′tər), *n.* **1** person from whom
one is descended, usually one more remote than a
grandparent; forefather. **2** a forerunner; precur-
sor. **3** the early form from which a species or
group is descended. [< Old French *ancestre*
< Latin *antecessor* < *antecedere* go before]

an ces tral (an ses′trəl), *adj.* of or inherited from
ancestors: *an ancestral home, an ancestral trait.*

au then tic (ô then′tik), *adj.* **1** worthy of accept-
ance, trust or belief; reliable: *an authentic account of the incident.* **2** coming from the source
stated; not copied; real: *A comparison of signa-
tures showed that the letter was authentic.*
[< Greek *authentikos* < *auto-* by oneself +
-hentēs one who acts] **—au then′ti cal ly,** *adv.*

bap tize (bap tīz′, bap′tīz), *v.t.,* **-tized, -tiz ing.**
1 dip (a person) into water or sprinkle with water
as a sign of washing away sin and admission into
the Christian church. **2** give a first name to (a
person) at baptism; christen. **3** give a name to;
name. **4** purify; cleanse. **5** introduce; initiate.
[< Greek *baptizein* < *baptein* to dip]

be stow (bi stō′), *v.t.* **1** give (something) as a gift;
give; confer. **2** make use of; apply.

car cass (kär′kəs), *n.* **1** body of a dead animal.
2 INFORMAL. a human body, dead or living (now
usually in ridicule or humor). **3** the shell or
framework of any structure, such as a building or
ship.

ca reen (kə rēn′), *v.i.* **1** lean to one side or sway
sharply; tilt; tip: *The ship careened in the strong
wind.* **2** rush headlong with a swaying motion;
lurch: *The car careened down the hill.* —*v.t.*
1 lay (a ship) over on one side for cleaning,
painting, repairing, etc. **2** cause to lean to one
side or sway sharply: *The gale careened the
sailboat.*

cen sus (sen′səs), *n.* an official count of the people of a country or district. It is taken to find out the number of people, their age, sex, occupation, and many other facts about them and their property. [< Latin < *censere* appraise]

chan de lier (shan′də lir′), *n.* a branched fixture for lights, usually hanging from the ceiling.

chron i cle (kron′ə kəl), *n., v.,* **-cled, -cling.** —*n.* **1** record of events in the order in which they took place; history; story. **2** narrative; account. —*v.t.* **1** write the history of; tell the story of. **2** put on record.

di aph a nous (dī af′ə nəs), *adj.* transparent: *Gauze is diaphanous.*

di vulge (də vulj′, dī vulj′), *v.t.,* **-vulged, -vulg ing.** make known or tell openly (something private or secret); reveal. —**di vulg′er,** *n.*

ex ult (eg zult′), *v.i.* be very glad; rejoice greatly.

ex ul ta tion (eg′zul tā′shən, ek′sul tā′shən), *n.* an exulting; great rejoicing; triumph.

fence (fens), *n., v.,* **fenced, fenc ing.** —*n.* **1** railing, wall, or similar barrier around a yard, garden, field, farm, etc., to mark a boundary or to prevent people or animals from going out or coming in. **2** person who buys and sells stolen goods. **3** place where stolen goods are bought and sold. **4 mend one's fences,** look after one's interests; promote good relations. **5 on the fence,** doubtful; hesitating. —*v.t.* put a fence around; keep out or in with a fence; enclose with a fence. —*v.i.* **1** fight with long, slender swords or foils. **2** evade giving answers or making admissions; parry questions.

friv o lous (friv′ə ləs), *adj.* **1** lacking in seriousness or sense; silly: *Frivolous behavior is out of place in a courtroom.* **2** of little worth or importance; trivial.

ge om e try (jē om′ə trē), *n., pl.* **-tries.** branch of mathematics which studies the relationship of points, lines, angles, and surfaces of figures in space; the mathematics of space. Geometry includes the definition, comparison, and measurement of squares, triangles, circles, cubes, cones, spheres, and other plane and solid figures. [< Greek *geōmetria* < *gē* earth + *-metria* measuring]

gim mick (gim′ik), *n.* SLANG. **1** any small device, especially one used secretly or in a tricky manner. **2** a hidden or tricky condition in a plan, etc.; catch. **3** idea, scheme, or stunt to attract attention. [origin unknown]

a	hat	oi	oil
ā	age	ou	out
ä	far	u	cup
e	let	ù	put
ē	equal	ü	rule
ėr	term		
i	it	ch	child
ī	ice	ng	long
o	hot	sh	she
ō	open	th	thin
ô	order	ᴛʜ	then
		zh	measure

ə = { a in about / e in taken / i in pencil / o in lemon / u in circus }

< = derived from

chandelier The **chandelier** dresses up the room.

glimpse (glimps), *n., v.,* **glimpsed, glimps ing.**
—*n.* **1** a short, quick view or look: *I caught a glimpse of the falls as our train went by.* **2** a short, faint appearance: *There was a glimpse of truth in what they said.* —*v.t.* catch a short, quick view of. —*v.i.* look quickly; glance.

gut tur al (gut′ər əl), *adj.* **1** of the throat. **2** formed in the throat; harsh: *speak in a deep, guttural voice.* **3** formed between the back of the tongue and the soft palate. The *g* in *go* is a guttural sound. —*n.* sound formed between the back of the tongue and the soft palate. The sound *k* is a guttural in the word *cool.*

hy brid (hī′brid), *n.* **1** offspring of two organisms of different varieties, species, races, etc. The mule is a hybrid of a female horse and a male donkey. **2** (in genetics) offspring of two individuals that differ in at least one gene. **3** anything of mixed origin. A word formed of parts from different languages is a hybrid. —*adj.* **1** bred from two different species, varieties, etc. A mule is a hybrid animal. **2** of mixed origin. [< Latin *hybrida*]

im part (im pärt′), *v.t.* **1** give a part or share of; give: *The new furnishings imparted an air of newness to the old house.* **2** communicate; tell: *They imparted the news of their engagement to their families.* —**im part′ment,** *n.*

in ci sive (in sī′siv), *adj.* **1** sharp or keen; penetrating; acute: *incisive criticism.* **2** incising; cutting.

in cred u lous (in krej′ə ləs), *adj.* **1** not ready to believe; doubting; skeptical: *If they look incredulous show them the evidence.* **2** showing a lack of belief: *an incredulous smile.* —**in cred′u lous-ly,** *adv.*

in gen ious (in jē′nyəs), *adj.* **1** skillful in making; good at inventing. **2** cleverly planned or made: *This mousetrap is an ingenious device.*

in her it (in her′it), *v.t.* **1** receive as an heir: *After his death his wife and children will inherit his property.* **2** receive from one's parents or ancestors through heredity: *inherit blue eyes.* **3** receive (anything) by succession from one who came before: *The new government inherited a financial crisis.* —*v.i.* succeed as an heir.

in tri cate (in′trə kit), *adj.* **1** with many twists and turns; puzzling, entangled, or complicated: *an intricate knot, an intricate plot.* **2** very hard to understand: *intricate directions.*

in tro ver sion (in′trə vėr′zhən, in′trə vėr′shən), *n.* tendency to be more interested in one's own thoughts and feelings than in what is going on around one; tendency to think rather than act.

intricate The ring has an **intricate** design.

in tro vert ed (in′trə vėr′tid), *adj.* characterized by introversion.

ir rel e vant (i rel′ə vənt), *adj.* not to the point; off the subject: *an irrelevant question.*

lu mi nous (lü′mə nəs), *adj.* **1** shining by its own light: *The sun and stars are luminous bodies.* **2** full of light; shining; bright. **3** easily understood; clear; enlightening.

me lo di ous (mə lō′dē əs), *adj.* **1** sweet-sounding; pleasing to the ear; musical; melodic; harmonious: *melodious verse.* **2** producing melody; singing sweetly: *melodious birds.* **3** having a melody; having to do with or of the nature of melody.

mo not o ny (mə not′n ē), *n.* **1** sameness of tone or pitch. **2** lack of variety. **3** wearisome sameness.

mud dy (mud′ē), *adj.,* **-di er, -di est. 1** of or like mud. **2** having much mud; covered with mud. **3** clouded with mud or any other sediment; turbid; cloudy: *muddy water, muddy coffee.* **4** not clear, pure, or bright; dull: *a muddy color.*

no ble (nō′bəl), *adj.,* **-bler, -blest. 1** high and great by birth, rank, or title; aristocratic: *a noble family, noble blood.* **2** high and great in character; showing greatness of mind; good; worthy: *a noble deed.* **3** having excellent qualities; fine: *a noble animal.* **4** grand in appearance; splendid; magnificent: *a noble sight.*

non cha lant (non′shə lənt, non′shə länt′), *adj.* without enthusiasm; coolly unconcerned; indifferent: *It was hard to remain nonchalant during all the excitement.* —**non′cha lant ly,** *adv.*

phlegm (flem), *n.* **1** the thick mucus discharged into the mouth and throat during a cold or other respiratory disease. **2** sluggish disposition or temperament; indifference. **3** coolness; calmness.

pres er va tion (prez′ər vā′shən), *n.* **1** a preserving; keeping safe: *the preservation of a historic building.* **2** a being preserved; being kept safe.

prod i gy (prod′ə jē), *n., pl.* **-gies. 1** person endowed with amazing brilliance, talent, etc., especially a remarkably talented child: *a musical prodigy.* **2** a marvelous example: *Samson performed prodigies of strength.* **3** a wonderful sign or omen: *An eclipse of the sun seemed a prodigy to early peoples.*

pro gress sion (prə gresh′ən), *n.* **1** a progressing; a moving forward; going ahead: *Creeping is a slow method of progression.* **2** (in mathematics) a sequence of quantities in which there is always the same relation between each quantity and the one succeeding it. 2, 4, 6, 8, 10 are in arithmetical progression. 2, 4, 8, 16, 32 are in geometrical progression.

a hat	oi oil
ā age	ou out
ä far	u cup
e let	ů put
ē equal	ü rule
ėr term	
i it	ch child
ī ice	ng long
o hot	sh she
ō open	th thin
ô order	ᴛʜ then
	zh measure

ə = {
a in about
e in taken
i in pencil
o in lemon
u in circus
}

< = derived from

prodigy The **prodigy** learned to play the cello at an early age.

ram i fi ca tion (ram′ə fə kā′shən), *n.* **1** a dividing or spreading out into branches or parts. **2** manner or result of branching; branch; part; subdivision.

re ject (*v.* ri jekt′; *n.* rē′jekt), *v.t.* **1** refuse to take, use, believe, consider, grant, etc.: *They rejected our help.* **2** throw away as useless or unsatisfactory: *Reject all apples with soft spots.* **3** repulse or rebuff (a person or an appeal). **4** vomit. **5** (of the body) to resist the introduction of (foreign tissue) by the mechanism of immunity. —*n.* a rejected person or thing. —**re ject′er,** *n.*

re jec tion (ri jek′shən), *n.* **1** act of rejecting. **2** condition of being rejected. **3** thing rejected. **4** immunological resistance of the body to the grafting or implantation of foreign tissue.

ro mance (rō mans′, rō′mans), *n.* **1** a love story. **2** story of adventure: *"The Arabian Nights" is a romance.* **3** a medieval story or poem telling of heroes: *romances about King Arthur.* **4** real events or conditions that are like such stories, full of love, excitement, or noble deeds; the character or quality of such events or conditions. **5** a love affair. **6** an extravagant or wild exaggeration; made-up story; falsehood: *Nobody believes her romances about her adventures.*

sheepish The boy looked **sheepish** when caught with his hand in the cookie jar.

scalp (skalp), *n.* **1** the skin on the top and back of the head, usually covered with hair. **2** part of this skin, formerly kept as a token of victory by certain American Indians. —*v.t.* **1** cut or tear the scalp from. **2** INFORMAL. **a** buy and sell to make small quick profits. **b** trade in (theater tickets, stocks, etc.) especially buying at face value and selling at higher prices. —*v.i.* INFORMAL. buy and sell theater tickets, stocks, etc., to make small quick profits. —**scalp′er,** *n.*

scram (skram), *v.i.,* **scrammed, scram ming.** SLANG. go at once. [short for *scramble*]

sheep ish (shē′pish), *adj.* **1** awkwardly bashful or embarrassed: *a sheepish smile.* **2** like a sheep; timid; weak; stupid.

sob (sob), *v.,* **sobbed, sob bing,** *n.* —*v.i.* **1** cry or sigh with short, quick breaths. **2** make a sound like a sob: *The wind sobbed.* —*v.t.* **1** put, send, etc., by sobbing: *sob oneself to sleep.* **2** utter with sobs: *sob out a sad story.* —*n.* **1** act of sobbing. **2** sound of sobbing or any sound like it.

spiel (spēl, shpēl), SLANG. —*n.* a talk; speech; harangue, especially one of a cheap, noisy nature. —*v.i., v.t.* talk; speak; say in or as a spiel. [< German *spielen* to play] —**spiel′er,** *n.*

sur name (sèr′nām′), *n., v.,* **-named, -nam ing.** —*n.* **1** a last name; family name. **2** name added to a person's real name: *William I of England had the surname "the Conqueror."* —*v.t.* give a surname to; call by a surname: *Simon was surnamed Peter.*

sus pect (v. sə spekt′; n. sus′pekt; adj. sus′pekt, sə spekt′), v.t. **1** imagine to be so; think likely: *suspected danger*. **2** believe guilty, false, bad, etc., without proof: *suspect someone of being a thief*. **3** feel no confidence in; doubt: *The judge suspected the truth of the defendant's alibi.* —v.i. be suspicious. —n. person suspected. —adj. open to or viewed with suspicion.

sym bol (sim′bəl), n. something that stands for or represents an idea, quality, condition, or other abstraction: *The lion is the symbol of courage; the lamb, of meekness; the olive branch, of peace; the cross, of Christianity.*

sym bol ic (sim bol′ik), adj. **1** used as a symbol: *A lily is symbolic of purity*. **2** of a symbol; expressed by a symbol or symbols; using symbols or symbolism: *a symbolic poem. Writing is a symbolic form of expression.*

te pee (tē′pē), n. tent used by the American Indians of the Great Plains, made of hides sewn together and stretched over poles arranged in the shape of a cone. Also, **teepee**. [< Sioux *tipi*]

ti′pi. *See* tepee.

tote (tōt), v., **tot ed, tot ing.** INFORMAL. —v.t. **1** carry; haul. **2** find the total or sum of; add or sum (*up*): *tote up a bill.*

tout (tout), INFORMAL. —v.t. **1** try to get (customers, jobs, votes, etc.). **2** urge betting on (a racehorse) by claiming to have special information. **3** BRITISH. spy out (information about racehorses). **4** praise highly and insistently.

tri um phant (trī um′fənt), adj. **1** victorious or successful: *a triumphant army*. **2** rejoicing because of victory or success.

un sus pect′ing. *See* suspect.

vi ce ver sa (vī′sə vėr′sə; vīs vėr′sə), the other way round; conversely: *John blamed Mary, and vice versa (Mary blamed John).* [< Latin]

a hat	oi oil
ā age	ou out
ä far	u cup
e let	u̇ put
ē equal	ü rule
ėr term	
i it	ch child
ī ice	ng long
o hot	sh she
ō open	th thin
ô order	ŦH then
	zh measure

ə = { a in about / e in taken / i in pencil / o in lemon / u in circus

< = derived from

tepee Many American Indians have lived in a **tepee**.

ACKNOWLEDGMENTS

Text

Page 7: "What Do I Do Now?" from *If This Is Love, I'll Take Spaghetti* by Ellen Conford. Copyright © 1983 by Ellen Conford. Reprinted by permission of Four Winds Press, an imprint of Macmillan Publishing Company.

Page 21: From *Why Me?* by Ellen Conford. Copyright © 1985 by Conford Enterprises Ltd. By permission of Little, Brown and Company.

Page 49: "Finding Myself" by Ellen Conford. Copyright © by Ellen Conford, 1991.

Page 52: "The Sidewalk Racer" by Lillian Morrison from *The Sidewalk Racer and Other Poems of Sports and Motion.* Copyright © 1965, 1967, 1968, 1977 by Lillian Morrison. Reprinted by permission of Marian Reiner for the author.

Page 53: "I'll Walk the Tightrope" by Margaret Danner. Reprinted with permission of Naomi Washington for the Estate of Margaret Danner.

Page 55: "The Fuller Brush Man" by Gloria D. Miklowitz from *Visions* by Donald R. Gallo, editor. Copyright © 1987 by Gloria D. Miklowitz. Used by permission of Dell Books, a division of Bantam Doubleday Dell Publishing Group, Inc.

Page 65: "Rules of the Game" from *The Joy Luck Club* by Amy Tan. Copyright © 1989 by Amy Tan. Reprinted by permission of The Putnam Publishing Group.

Page 83: "All the Names of Baby Hag" by Patricia MacLachlan. Copyright © 1986 by Patricia MacLachlan. From *Dragons & Dreams: A Collection of New Fantasy and Science Fiction Stories* edited by Jane Yolen, Martin H. Greenberg, and Charles G. Waugh. Copyright © 1986 by Jane Yolen, Martin H. Greenberg, and Charles G. Waugh. Reprinted by permission of HarperCollins Publishers.

Page 95: "How Do Story Ideas Begin?" by Patricia MacLachlan. Copyright © by Patricia MacLachlan, 1991.

Page 98: "The Naming of Cats" from *Old Possum's Book of Practical Cats.* Copyright © 1939 by T.S. Eliot and renewed 1967 by Esme Valerie Eliot. Reprinted by permission of Harcourt Brace Jovanovich, Inc.

Page 101: Excerpt from *Roots* by Alex Haley. Copyright © 1976 by Alex Haley. Used by permission of Doubleday, a division of Bantam Doubleday Dell Publishing Group, Inc.

Page 117: "My Name" from *The House on Mango Street* by Sandra Cisneros. Copyright © 1989 by Sandra Cisneros. Published by Vintage Books, a division of Random House, Inc., NY. Reprinted by permission of Susan Bergholz Literary Services, NYC, NY.

Page 121: "First Names Around the World" from *Your Name—All About It* by Mary Price Lee. Copyright © 1980 by Mary Price Lee. Reprinted by permission of Westminster/John Knox Press.

Page 131: "Far Looker" by Mari Sandoz from *Hostiles and Friendlies: Selected Short Writings of Mari Sandoz.* Copyright © 1959 by the University of Nebraska Press. Copyright renewed 1987 by Caroline Sandoz Pifer. Reprinted by permission of McIntosh and Otis, Inc.

Page 133: "Name Giveaway" by Phillip William George from *The Next World: Poems by 32 Third World Americans* edited by Joseph Bruchac. Copyright © 1978 by Joseph Bruchac. Reprinted by permission.

Artists

Illustrations owned and copyrighted by the illustrator.

Marc Rosenthal: Cover, 1, 3–5, 136–137
John Kleber: 6, 12, 19
Michael Paraskevas: 20, 31, 44, 47, 51
Jon Stepping: 52, 53
David Wariner: 54, 58–59, 63
Stephán Daigle: 64, 68, 70, 73, 75, 77
John Sanford: 82, 83, 86, 88, 93, 97
Naomi Spellman: 94
Mary Lynn Blasutta: 120, 121–129
Robin Moore: 130, 131

Photographs

Page 48: Courtesy of Ellen Conford
Page 94: Courtesy of Patricia MacLachlan
Pages 100, 105, 111: Reprinted by permission of Ebony Magazine, © 1977 Johnson Publishing Company, Inc.
Page 116: Courtesy Institute of Texan Cultures, University of Texas

Glossary

The contents of the Glossary entries in this book have been adapted from Scott Foresman *Advanced Dictionary,* copyright © 1988 by Scott, Foresman and Company.

Page 139: "Green Room" 1964, Courtesy of the White House Historical Association; Page 143: Lynn M. Stone
Unless otherwise acknowledged, all photographs are the property of Scott-Foresman.